COMBATING BURGLARY:
AN EVALUATION OF THREE STRATEGIES

Janet E. Stockdale & Peter J. Gresham

POLICE RESEARCH GROUP
CRIME DETECTION AND PREVENTION SERIES: PAPER NO 59
LONDON: HOME OFFICE POLICE DEPARTMENT

Editor: Barry Webb
Home Office Police Research Group
50 Queen Anne's Gate
London SW1H 9AT

Police Research Group: Crime Detection and Prevention Series

The Home Office Police Research Group (PRG) was formed in 1992 to carry out and manage research relevant to the work of the police service. The terms of reference for the Group include the requirement to identify and disseminate good policing practice.

The Crime Detection and Prevention Series follows on from the Crime Prevention Unit papers, a series which has been published by the Home Office since 1983. The recognition that effective crime strategies will often involve both crime prevention and crime investigation, however, has led to the scope of this series being broadened. This new series will present research material on both crime prevention and crime detection in a way which informs policy and practice throughout the service.

A parallel series of papers on resource management and organisational issues is also published by PRG, as is a periodical on policing research called 'Focus'.

ISBN 1-85893-344-7

Foreword

In its recent review of crime management in police forces, the Audit Commission emphasised the need to move away from the current predominantly reactive approach to offences of burglary and motor vehicle crime to more proactive operations, making greater use of intelligence to target prolific and serious offenders. Operation Bumblebee was cited as an example of the approach being advocated, and other forces have adopted similar approaches to burglary - either as force-wide or more locally designed strategies.

This report takes an in-depth look at the approaches implemented in three forces - Operation Bumblebee in the Metropolitan Police, Operation Gemini in Gloucestershire which shares some of the objectives and characteristics of Bumblebee, and the changes arising from a review of crime investigation and the CID in Hampshire which did not include high profile use of the media. The study shows that burglaries have reduced after each of the strategies was introduced, providing a *prima facie* case for giving the strategies some of the credit. The study goes on to pick out the circumstances in which such proactive strategies seem most likely to be effective and considers in particular the contribution strategic use of the media can make.

The report lists a number of key elements in these strategies. The success of the strategies in reducing burglary could be due to the triggering of any of a number of mechanisms, for example deterring offenders by convincing them that their risk of capture has increased or reducing the activity of prolific burglars by increasing their detection. Further work currently underway as part of PRG's Police Operations Against Crime programme will address the extent to which the second of these mechanisms can be achieved by proactive, intelligence-based operations against burglary. Together with this study, this work will add greatly to our understanding of what can be achieved by such strategies and how they might be designed and implemented to achieve maximum effect.

I M BURNS
Deputy Under Secretary of State
Police Department
Home Office
December 1994

Acknowledgements

We would like to express our thanks and appreciation to all those who have contributed to this research. Fundamental to the progress of the project so far has been the co-operation we received from the three police services involved in the research: The Metropolitan Police, Gloucestershire Constabulary and Hampshire and Isle of Wight Constabulary. We are especially grateful to the officers of all ranks who have given so freely of their time and ideas and to the liaison officer in each of the services who provided invaluable practical help and guidance.

JE Stockdale and PJ Gresham

The Authors

Dr Janet Stockdale is senior lecturer in Social Psychology at the London School of Economics and Political Science.

Peter Gresham is a social and economic research consultant (Urbecon Ltd).

Executive summary

Burglary, especially domestic burglary, has become an increasing source of concern to the police and to the public, both in London and in the shire counties. This has led to police forces adopting a variety of strategies for combating burglary and this report describes an evaluation of three such strategies.

Operation Bumblebee, adopted by the Metropolitan Police Service (MPS), is a high profile anti-burglary strategy. Operation Gemini, introduced by Gloucestershire Constabulary, is directed at both burglary and motor-vehicle crime and some of its features are similar to those of Operation Bumblebee. Hampshire Constabulary has not adopted a high profile strategy for dealing with burglary, but has implemented organisational and procedural changes which are designed to affect its response to burglary and other crime.

The aims of the research were to evaluate the impact of the three approaches and to identify the implications for good practice in the prevention and detection of burglary.

The study drew on statistics for burglary and certain other categories of offence, documentary material and interviews with 169 officers of all ranks and other relevant personnel.

The first phase of the research identified the key elements of each strategy and the associated structural and procedural changes. The second phase examined officers' responses to the strategies and the implementation process and assessed the effects on operational practice and service delivery. The third phase evaluated the extent to which the strategies are associated with improvements in police operations and performance.

The analysis of each strategy demonstrated commonalities in approach, with all three strategies adopting a more proactive, intelligence-based response to burglary. Variations in implementation reflected the clarity and coherence of the strategy, the size and structure of the force, and the tensions between central and local control over the setting of priorities and resource allocation. A defined, high profile burglary strategy resulted in greater uniformity in working practices.

In all three cases, performance was seen to have benefited from the greater use of intelligence and targeting of offenders, and the allocation of resources. Dedicated squads were seen as important to the success of both Operations Bumblebee and Gemini.

There were other factors associated with the perceived success of the high profile anti-burglary strategies. Many of these derived from the publicity campaigns, an integral part of the strategies, and resulting media coverage, which had affected both public perceptions and police commitment. Lack of resources was identified as the major factor which constrained the police response to burglary.

The introduction of each of the three strategies is associated with improved performance with respect to burglary. The results associated with the Metropolitan Police Service's Operation Bumblebee are particularly striking and appear to be being sustained. Since the introduction of Met-wide Bumblebee, the incidence of recorded burglary has reduced significantly and both the number and proportion of burglary offences solved have increased. Much of the increase in detections for burglary derives from secondary detections, especially those resulting from post-sentence visits, rather than from primary detections. Following the introduction of Operation Gemini and other changes in crime management in Gloucestershire, the incidence of burglary has decreased. The effect appeared to be restricted to primarily urban areas initially, although there is now evidence of a reduction in rural areas. More recently there are signs of an increase in detections for burglary, particularly by primary means. In Hampshire, the structural and procedural changes have been slower to take effect, but there is now some evidence of a reduction in burglary comparable to that found in the Metropolitan Police District (MPD). There is also some indication of an increase in the number of secondary detections for burglary offences.

It should be recognised that many of the factors that govern crime levels lie outside the ambit of police control and that the reduction in recorded burglaries is likely to be multiply-determined. However, innovative strategies which contain certain key elements can contribute to the control and management of burglary. The evidence of an increasing reliance on secondary detections, especially those deriving from post-sentence visits, raises questions about the relative merits of primary and secondary detections, their associated resource demands and their implications for both offenders and victims.

The analysis of the strategies and their impact - not only on crime figures but on the officers involved in service delivery - raises a number of issues about the management and resourcing of an anti-burglary strategy. These must be addressed if such a strategy is to be sustainable in the long-term, to retain the support of officers and to meet the needs of the community it seeks to serve.

There are clear implications for good practice in the prevention and detection of burglary and more generally. A high profile strategy with a well-publicised 'brand name' can be effective in gaining the support of the public and other agencies, and of the police themselves, but requires careful implementation. Attention needs to be paid to internal communications, training needs, resource availability and deployment, and the positioning of the strategy in relation to other force-wide and local priorities. 'Brand names' complement both the shift in strategy towards a proactive, rather than simply a reactive approach, based on the use of criminal intelligence to target active criminals, and the move toward more effective crime management and resource allocation.

The initial evidence suggest that strategies which are based on the principles of proactive, intelligence-led policing - both those which use a high profile, targeted approach and those which adopt a more global analysis - can contribute to the control and management of burglary and other high-volume crime. The choice of strategy will depend upon the scale and distribution of the problem of burglary, the range of local problems and priorities, resource availability and associated demands, and variability in policing contexts. High profile strategies, supported by publicity and community links, can bring added value to efforts directed at crime prevention and detection. Such strategies can be an effective use of resources, can improve the quality of service given to the public and help to convey the message that crime is a community, not just a police problem.

Contents

Page

Foreword (iii)

Acknowledgements (iv)

Executive summary (v)

List of tables (ix)

List of figures (x)

1. Introduction 1

    The problem of burglary 1
    The research 2
    Structure of the report 5

2. Strategy: development and implementation 6

    Operation Bumblebee in the Metropolitan Police Service 6
    Operation Gemini in Gloucestershire Constabulary 11
    Hampshire Constabulary's strategy for dealing with burglary 14

3. Assessment: how do the three strategies compare? 17

    Impact on burglary and other offences 17
    Police perspectives and level of support 39
    Other benefits 51
    Drawbacks 53

4. Implications for good practice 56

5. Conclusions 63

References 66

PRG Research Papers 67

List of Tables

Table No.	Caption	Page
1	Number of clear-ups and percentage change in number of clear-ups: MPD 7-month period (June to December) 1991-1993, burglary all, dwelling and non-dwelling	19
2	Number of clear-ups and percentage change in number of clear-ups: Gloucestershire 7-month period (June to December) 1990-1993, burglary all, dwelling and non-dwelling	25
3	Number of clear-ups and percentage change in number of clear-ups: Hampshire 12-month period (January to December) 1991-1993, burglary all, dwelling and non-dwelling.	29
4	Clear-up rate (%) and number of clear-ups for burglary (all) in MPS, Gloucestershire and Hampshire: June to December (MPS & Glocs), January to December (Hants)	31
5	Officers' views: most important actions by police and public to combat burglary	40
6	Elements of current strategy: frequency of occurrence in the three forces	43
7	Positive impact of the three strategies: number (n) and percentage (%) of officers who expressed a positive view (officers below the rank of chief inspector)	48
8	Officers' views: key factors contributing to success in the three forces	49
9	Officers' views: constraints on success in the three forces	50

List of Figures

Figure No.	Caption	Page
1	Recorded burglary incidence all, dwelling and non-dwelling in MPD: 7-month period (June to December) 1991-1993	18
2	Clear-up rates in MPD: 7-month period (June-December) 1991-1993, burglary all, dwelling and non-dwelling	19
3	Clear-ups: all burglary, MPD 7-month period June - December 1991-1993	20
4a	Origins of burglary clear-ups, MPD: 7-month period June - December 1991	22
4b	Origins of burglary clear-ups, MPD: 7-month period June - December 1992	22
4c	Origins of burglary clear-ups, MPD: 7-month period June - December 1993	22
5	Recorded burglary incidence all, dwelling and non-dwelling: Gloucestershire 7-month period (June to December) 1990-1993	24
6	Clear-up rates for burglary all, dwelling and non-dwelling Gloucestershire: 7-month period (June-December) 1990-1993	25
7	Recorded burglary incidence all, dwelling and non-dwelling: Hampshire yearly period (January to December) 1991-1993	27
8	Clear-up rates for burglary all, dwelling and non-dwelling Hampshire: 12-month period (January-December) 1991-1993	28
9	Recorded burglary incidence (all) in MPS, Gloucestershire and Hampshire: June-December (MPS & Glocs) January-December (Hants)	31

1. Introduction

The problem of burglary

Burglary, especially burglary dwelling or domestic burglary, has become an increasing source of concern to the police and to the public, both in cities and in the shire counties. Home Office statistics indicate that of the 5.4 million crimes (excluding criminal damage under £20) recorded by the police in England and Wales in 1992, 25 percent were burglary - second in volume only to thefts of and from cars (29%) (Home Office, 1993). The incidence of burglary has shown a significant increase over recent years, with burglary dwelling showing an increase of 78 percent over the period 1982-92. This compares with an increase in total recorded crime of 74 percent over the same ten-year period.

Over the year 1991-92 the percentage increase in burglary was 11 percent, the second highest proportionate increase in recorded crime and only marginally lower than the increase for criminal damage (11.5%). Although the risk of burglary varies across type of neighbourhood, with the highest risk being in the poorest areas, the risk of being a victim of burglary in England and Wales is one of the highest in Europe.

Crime survey data suggest that, although the majority of burglary offences committed are reported (73%), under half are recorded (46%), one in ten is cleared up (11%) and three in every hundred results in a caution or a conviction. The clear-up rate for burglaries recorded by the police in 1992 was 20 percent, compared with a clear-up rate for all crimes of 26 percent. The clear-up or detection rate has to be seen in the context of increasing crime levels and consequent increase in workload. Although there have been increases both in the number of crimes cleared up (23%) and in productivity (16%) - as indexed by clear-ups per officer - over the period 1982-92, the dramatic rise in recorded crime over the same time period (74%) has resulted in a decline in the overall clear-up or detection rate from 37 percent to its 1992 level (26%).

The rising incidence of crime, including burglary, has had an impact on public perceptions and fear of crime. A recent poll of over 2,000 adults (conducted by MORI, 1994) found that ninety-three percent of those interviewed believed that crime had increased over the past few years - a perception borne out by the statistics - and the same percentage reported that their concern about crime had increased over the past few years. Having their home burgled was the crime people feared most (77%) and fear of having their homes or possessions vandalised ranked second (56%). Similar results emerged from a public attitude survey, commissioned by Hampshire Constabulary in 1992, which identified property crime - burglaries/break-ins and vandalism/damage - as the most important local policing priority.

Such findings indicate that burglary has increasingly become a 'fact of life' both for the public who experience its effects and for the police who are responsible for its investigation.

The research

Concern about burglary has led to the police service adopting a variety of approaches to deal with the problem. This report describes an evaluation of the strategies for combating burglary in three police forces: the Metropolitan Police Service (MPS), Gloucestershire Constabulary and the Hampshire and Isle of Wight Constabulary.

The aims of the research were to evaluate the implementation and effectiveness of three approaches to combating burglary and to identify the implications for good practice in the prevention and detection of burglary. The first phase of the research identified the key elements of each strategy and the associated structural and procedural changes. The second phase examined officers' responses to the strategies and the implementation process, and assessed the effects on operational practice and service delivery. The third phase evaluated the extent to which the strategies have improved police operations and performance.

The research involves an examination of Operation Bumblebee within the MPS and a comparison between this strategic approach and those operating in two other forces. Gloucestershire Constabulary has introduced Operation Gemini, some of the aims and characteristics of which are similar to those of Operation Bumblebee. Hampshire Constabulary has not adopted a high profile strategy for dealing with burglary on a force-wide basis but has implemented organisational and procedural changes based on a review of the investigation of crime and the CID.

The three forces examined have had varying experiences in recent years. In London, the number of reported burglaries has doubled over the past twenty years and the percentage of offences solved has declined. However, in 1992-93 the steady rise in burglaries in London was halted, with the number of reported burglaries showing a fall by one percent compared with the previous year. Also the detection rate for burglary increased from 10 to 12 percent. These improvements were attributed to the MPS's anti-burglary strategy which was pioneered in North London.

In Gloucestershire, recorded crime grew steadily during the 1980s, but the rise was spectacular in the early 1990s - 21 percent in 1990 and 32 percent in 1991. In 1992, a third of all recorded crimes related to property and more than a quarter were burglary offences. While detections rose in absolute terms from 1982-92, the detection rate fell from 42 percent to 24 percent. The detection rate for burglary was 15 percent in 1992 (Gloucestershire Constabulary, 1992). In Hampshire, recorded crime rose by 7 percent in 1991/92 while the incidence of burglary rose by 8 percent and domestic burglary by 11 percent. The detection rate for burglary fell from 20 percent in 1991 to 17 percent in 1992 (Hampshire Constabulary, 1992).

Data sources

The analysis of the strategy implementation and its impact was based on:

- interviews with a structured sample of officers of all ranks in the three forces
- an examination of relevant documentation supplied by the three forces
- an analysis of data relating to recorded crime and clear-ups in the three forces

The information was considered in the context of other factors which may have influenced the incidence and investigation of crime. Determination of cause and effect is difficult to ascertain with complete certainty. Changes in performance which occur concurrent with or subsequent to changes in strategy may be attributable to internal management or procedural changes other than those under scrutiny. Equally, they may be due to exogenous factors, such as changes in levels of socio-economic deprivation (cf. Field, 1990). However, such external contextual effects apply to all the forces under consideration and a comparison of the relative performance levels across the three strategies will identify whether differential patterns exist which can be attributed to the introduction of a new strategy or to other internal changes.

The evaluation, especially that relating to the crime statistics, was necessarily constrained by its timing. All three strategies were of recent application when the data were collected: both Met-wide Bumblebee and the re-launched Operation Gemini (Gemini II) had been in operation for only seven months and the changes in Hampshire's approach had been implemented over a period of just more than a year. The conclusions drawn must be seen in the light of this constraint; a follow-up evaluation of the strategies will be necessary to assess their long-term impact and cost-effectiveness.

The interviews

The interviews provide an overview of officers' understanding of their respective force's approach to the problem of burglary and their perceptions of its implementation and effectiveness. In total, 169 officers and other relevant personnel were interviewed. Within each force, the sample comprised a cross-section of officers reflecting the local organisational structure and representing a variety of functions and specialisms.

MPS: the sample (n=84) was drawn from two of the eight areas in the Metropolitan Police District (MPD). The two areas selected, 1 and 4 Area, were each represented by two divisions such that the sample provided the basis for both area comparisons and divisional comparisons within areas.

Gloucestershire Constabulary: the sample (n=46) was drawn from two of the county's five divisions.

Hampshire Constabulary: the sample (n=39) comprised officers from four sub-divisions, three representing the force's three divisions on the mainland, and the fourth being the Isle of Wight sub-division.

The interview schedules took account of the responsibilities and expertise of the interviewee but, in some cases, operational constraints or lack of detailed knowledge precluded full answers. The interview schedule for Chief Inspectors and above, which focused on broader issues of strategy development and implementation, led to more wide-ranging discussion and less quantifiable responses. Officers below this level provided the bulk of the interview sample (83%) and some of the numerical data provided refer only to this sub-sample.

Questionnaires were sent to the six Metropolitan Police areas not participating in the study and to the three divisions in Gloucestershire which were not sampled. Completed questionnaires were returned by three of the six MPD areas (2, 5 and 7 Area) and by all three of the Gloucestershire divisions. The interview and questionnaire data were supplemented by the examination of any relevant documentation and the authors attended certain police operations as observers.

Crime statistics

All three forces supplied incidence and detection statistics for burglary and selected other offences, for a minimum of a three-year period. In some cases it was not possible to provide all the data requested, or in a particular format, and the analyses reflect these constraints. The analysis of the crime statistics focuses on samples of comparable data from periods before and after the introduction of strategy changes for combating burglary.

Criteria for assessment

The key question to be asked of the anti-burglary strategy adopted by each of the three forces under scrutiny is, 'Does the strategy work?' More specifically, does it have a positive impact on the incidence of burglary and/or detection? Does it bring other benefits? Do the benefits outweigh the costs? The issue is more complex than simple measures of recorded crime and clear-up rates since each strategy has other important, often longer-term and less tangible, aims, such as providing an enhanced quality of service to victims of burglary, improving co-operation between the police, public and other agencies, raising police morale and commitment, and increasing the value for money given by the police service.

Four domains were identified for evaluation:

i. **Impact on burglary and other offences.**
   What is the impact upon recorded crime and its detection? Are the strategies associated with a reduction in the incidence of burglary and/or an increase in the number of offences solved? Is there any evidence of displacement of criminal activity?

ii. **Police perspectives and level of support.**
   How were the changes in strategy perceived by the officers involved? Did the anti-burglary strategies gain the support of officers concerned with burglary?

iii. **Additional benefits.**
   Has a change in strategy brought any other benefits, such as more effective work practices or improvements in the quality of service to the public? What, if any, is the added value of publicity campaigns and media coverage?

iv. **Drawbacks.**
   What, if any, are the negative effects of an anti-burglary strategy? Does it have an adverse impact on other areas of police activity? What are the effects of prioritising burglary on resource allocation and what are the associated financial costs? Is a high profile anti-burglary strategy sustainable?

Structure of the report

Section 2 of the report outlines the origins and implementation of the anti-burglary strategies adopted in each of the three forces. Section 3 provides an evaluation of the strategies in terms of the assessment criteria, including an examination of officers' responses to the strategies and their implementation, and their effects on working practices and service delivery. Implications for good practice are identified in Section 4. Finally, Section 5 sets out the conclusions reached about the efficacy of the strategies and their future development.

2. Strategy: development and implementation

Operation Bumblebee in the Metropolitan Police Service

Origins

Operation Bumblebee began on 1 Area of the MPD on 1 June 1991. 1 Area covers some 134 square miles of varied development, ranging from inner city to semi-rural, and is policed by ten divisions each under the command of a chief superintendent. The total population is in excess of 1.25 million and is served by eight local authorities.

A continued growth in the number of burglary offences committed, a decrease in the proportion of offences solved, evidence that burglary was the crime local residents feared the most, combined with what appeared to be a fatalistic approach to the investigation of most house burglaries, provided the context for Operation Bumblebee. It was felt to be imperative to unite the police and public in a high-profile campaign against burglary.

The objectives of Operation Bumblebee were to:
- prevent burglary
- arrest and convict those responsible
- provide an enhanced quality of service to victims

The success of Operation Bumblebee, which drew on a previous initiative directed at reducing burglary artifice, was seen to depend on improvements in administration, intelligence, proactivity and crime prevention. In some cases the policies and procedures adopted under the auspices of Bumblebee were merely a formalisation of what had already been introduced. In other cases the reorganisation and working practices were new and were designed to introduce or extend good practice. No additional funding was made available, all expenses being met from existing budgets.

Introduction of Met-wide Bumblebee

Following the apparent success of Operation Bumblebee on 1 Area, and its subsequent introduction on 3 and 5 Areas, the decision was taken to extend the anti-burglary operation across all eight areas of the MPD. Operation Bumblebee was launched Met-wide in June 1993, with the strategic aim of improving the performance of the MPS with respect to burglary. A central theme of the operation was police-led co-operation with other components of the Criminal Justice System (CJS), central and local government, statutory and voluntary agencies, the commercial sector, the press and other media, the education sector and the public.

The operation was centrally led with overall co-ordination the responsibility of the MPS-wide steering group, led by a Commander and supported by local area co-ordinators. Although there were some prescriptive elements, including the requirement to make an impact on burglary, participate in co-ordinated searches, and take action against handlers of stolen property, there was also the capacity for local flexibility. It was recommended that the 1 Area model - an area burglary team and divisional burglary or 'Bumblebee' squads - should be adopted by all areas. However, the devolution of operational control to areas and divisions precluded making this a requirement.

The key elements of Met-wide Bumblebee

- **service-wide operations**
  * co-ordinated searches
  * area operations against burglars and handlers
  * Bumblebee property and crime prevention roadshow

- **publicity**
  * specific actions by Department of Public Affairs (DPA) eg. poster and leaflet campaign, publicity packs, media interviews/observing operations, publicity for major campaigns and promoting Operation Bumblebee and its logo
  * links with key organisations and agencies
  * internal newsletters (quarterly Met-wide and monthly on area)

- **prevention**
  * burglary artifice ('doorstoppers') code of practice (launched October 1993)
  * action to avoid repeat victimisation (eg. appropriate tasking and resourcing of Crime Prevention Officers (CPOs), targeting victims within 7 days of first burglary and monitoring of repeat victimisations)
  * community policing/partnership approach (eg. liaison with Neighbourhood Watch, schools, local authorities - to design out burglary - and other key agencies)
  * property identification initiatives (eg. property marking campaign, film processing company to offer reduce rates for processing photographs of valuable property)

- **improved investigation and detection**
  * intelligence (eg. assess/improve crime analysis capability, promote use of informants)
  * identification and dissemination of best practice (eg. preparation of burglary manual, post-sentence visits (PSVs), monitoring of innovation)
  * other support (eg. increase provision of fingerprint identifications and forensic evidence)

- **performance measurement**
  - * costing (police officers employed on full-day basis on Operation Bumblebee)
  - * evaluation of effectiveness (internal and external)
  - * victim care (promotion/assessment of improved sensitivity to victims' needs)
  - * maintenance of standards and ethics

Many elements of Met-wide Bumblebee replicate those pioneered on 1 Area, while others are innovative. Co-ordinated searches, or 'mass raids', remain a focus for police activity and media publicity. Recent initiatives include the Bumblebee Roadshows which, as well as displaying stolen property - some 2,000 items worth more than £2 million at the first Roadshow in central London - provide advice on a number of issues related to burglary, such as general crime prevention, photographing valuable property, property marking, Neighbourhood Watch and Victim Support.

Costing of Operation Bumblebee

Early estimates for the next financial year of the anticipated 'opportunity costs' associated with all service-wide activity against burglary are in the region of £36 million. This figure is based upon the costs of officers engaged on a specific Bumblebee activity or in a dedicated squad for a full working day only and takes no account of part days spent on work associated with Bumblebee or which is otherwise related to burglary. However, much of this money would have been spent in the normal course of events on officers carrying out the full range of police work, including dealing with burglary. Therefore such costings do not adequately quantify either the additional, marginal costs of Operation Bumblebee or the value of resources transferred to the operation from other police work. Neither do they identify those areas of activity which may have been adversely affected.

The other major costs incurred relate to the publicity campaigns, including the outdoor advertising campaigns, a targeted leaflet drop to 1.3 million homes and local campaigns and initiatives. The cost of these campaigns is in the region of £500,000 but again it has not proved possible to quantify the additional expenditure which has resulted from Operation Bumblebee.

Current implementation of Operation Bumblebee on 1 Area

When Operation Bumblebee was formally launched Met-wide, the 1 Area steering group was enhanced to include representatives from all ten divisions, as well as CPOs and community liaison officers. The Area Bumblebee team remains responsible for targeting burglars who cross divisional boundaries and handlers of stolen property and also co-ordinates area activity on combined operations.

<u>1 Area activities 1 October 1993 to 31 January 1994</u>

In order to combat the seasonal increase in burglary, 1 Area initiated a number of activities designed to complement those on divisions.

Stop and speak: A core element of the area co-ordinated activity was a stop and speak campaign, whereby officers stopped and spoke to people in the vicinity of an area where burglaries were known to be committed, to create the impression of intense police activity. The stop information was collated by the local intelligence officer (LIO) and forwarded to the area burglary unit.

Curfew monitoring: When an offender was bailed by the court, the Crown Prosecution Service (CPS) was asked to seek a curfew to cover the time-period of the offence, and a condition of residence. Burglary teams then visited offenders subject to a curfew to establish whether they were complying with their bail condition.

Audible warning: When a number of burglaries had occurred in a given location, residents were warned using the public address system on a police vehicle.

Other initiatives included: targeting of known burglars by traffic division; increased liaison with neighbourhood watches; and, targeting of car boot sales.

<u>Implementation on Chingford and Holloway divisions</u>

Chingford division has adopted the recommended model for the investigation of burglary. It has a divisional burglary team, comprising fifteen officers (a detective sergeant, four detective constables, six crime squad officers, three officers attached from sector, and one analyst).

In response to Operation Bumblebee, Holloway division initially established a divisional burglary squad and three sector CID teams, all based at one location and served by a centralised crime desk. After six months it was felt that these arrangements failed to satisfy local needs and a review of sector policing and the CID was conducted. The results of this review, combined with the preliminary results of a study of sector policing on Holloway division (Dixon and Stanko, 1993), formed the basis for a new structure, implemented in April 1993. The centralised crime and burglary squads were disbanded. CID was devolved to sector, with CID officers, Trainee Investigators (TIs) and uniformed officers on plain clothes attachment working in teams from the three sector bases. Crime desks were also established at each sector base. On each sector there are now two CID teams, one of which is designated as reactive and deals with work generated by the crime desk, and the other is proactive responding to tasks generated locally or by the intelligence cell.

Within the Bumblebee framework, all divisions are encouraged to mount initiatives designed to deal with local problems of burglary. Holloway division, for example, has undertaken a number of crime prevention initiatives, many of them in partnership with the local authority, and has mounted local anti-burglary operations.

Implementation of Operation Bumblebee on 4 Area

Context

4 Area stretches from the South bank of the Thames to the southern boundary of the MPD, on the borders of Surrey. It encompasses both inner city and suburban areas and therefore offers a range of social and economic contrasts similar to those found in 1 Area. The two sample divisions, Streatham and Croydon, are broadly representative of the different policing circumstances in 4 Area. So far as burglary is concerned, the two divisions show markedly different characteristics. On Streatham division, burglary is a largely localised and opportunistic crime. Croydon, on the other hand, provides an affluent target for mobile criminals. However, the two divisions had begun to adopt similar proactive approaches to dealing with burglary prior to Operation Bumblebee.

The introduction of Operation Bumblebee

When Met-wide Bumblebee was officially heralded in a briefing paper prepared by the Bumblebee co-ordinator for 4 Area (a detective superintendent), some of the methods and procedures associated with Bumblebee were already in use and others were in the process of introduction. The memorandum set out a list of some seventy-two specific tasks, changes of procedure and general guidelines for future activities designed to extend good practice and meet the expectations of the campaign. These included:

- Targeting of burglary across a range of police operations - for example, at least 50% of the time of surveillance teams should be directed towards burglary.
- Informants to be advised that priority would be given to burglary and additional funds made available (through virements from other divisional budgets) to increase rewards.
- Sector officers to be given specific targets to provide up-to-date intelligence - an 'adopt a burglar' scheme.
- An instruction that burglars' premises should be searched following arrest - such searches to be conducted both within the confines of PACE and on an ethically correct basis.

- A series of actions to raise the profile of police operations against burglary and promotion of the Operation Bumblebee logo and theme.

The major organisational changes required by Operation Bumblebee - the establishment of an area burglary squad and dedicated burglary squads on each division - had already been implemented on 4 Area to some degree. The area crime squad, which was already in existence, was designated the area burglary squad (although it is still referred to as the crime squad) and increased in size. The squad, which was co-located with the area Territorial Support Group (TSG), comprised eight detective constables drawn from the CID (one per division) and twelve officers from the TSG, led by a detective inspector. The squad was directed to act in a proactive role, targeting known criminals, especially prolific local burglars, or high risk areas, backed up by surveillance teams and other services such as forensic science and criminal intelligence. The squad would mount its own operations but, when required, would also provide support to divisions and supply officers to assist with major operations.

Croydon division had abolished its crime squad and put all available resources into a dedicated burglary team led by a detective inspector. In Streatham, a burglary squad had been created but the division had retained its crime squad and intelligence cell. In both cases, the burglary squads were seen as having both an investigative, or reactive, function and a proactive role, but the need to respond to reported crime inevitably means the reactive role will frequently take precedence. In Croydon, contacts with local community and business organisations led to a measure of commercial sponsorship.

Operation Gemini in Gloucestershire Constabulary

Context

Gloucestershire is a predominantly rural, sparsely populated county, with an area of 264,000 hectares and a population of just over half a million. It contains two urban centres, the City of Gloucester and the Borough of Cheltenham, which together account for 40 percent of the population of the county. Gloucestershire Constabulary has an establishment of 1,184 officers and 496 civilian staff. Gloucester and Cotswold divisions provide a good cross-section of the police service in the county. Gloucester division is primarily urban, compact and densely populated with ninety thousand people living in an area of only 3,300 hectares. Cotswold division is large and rural with a population of about seventy-three thousand spread over 114,000 hectares, almost a third of the county.

The evolution of Operation Gemini

Operation Gemini, although bearing certain similarities to Operation Bumblebee in the MPS, has its own distinct identity and distinguishing features. Like Bumblebee,

Gemini is targeted at burglary, but is also concerned with motor-vehicle crime, a significant and growing problem in Gloucestershire. Operation Gemini has had two distinct and separate phases: Gemini I and Gemini II.

Gemini I

The first phase, Gemini I, was originally conceived as a short term, experimental operation and was run for a three month period from November 1992 to January 1993. Gemini I was a response to the significant increases in high volume crime, particularly vehicle crime and burglary, over the last decade and to the recent sharp decline in clear-up rates. Its aim was 'to significantly reduce the rate of reported crime and increase the number of crime detections, focusing primarily, but not exclusively, on offences of house burglary, theft from motor vehicles and theft/taking without owner's consent (TWOC) of motor vehicles'.

Key elements of Gemini I

- A publicity campaign, including regular press statements and radio interviews.
- The creation of dedicated 'Gemini Units' of approximately 38 officers, under the command of an Inspector, in each of the (then) two divisions and provision of an additional overtime budget of £7,000.
- The adoption of 'high profile' publicly visible policing methods.
- Targeting of resources and operations on the basis of criminal intelligence and crime pattern analysis (CPA).
- The establishment of a headquarters-based force-wide steering group (led by the force co-ordinator) and introduction of continuous monitoring of performance.

An internal evaluation of the operation concluded that it had been successful. Although the incidence of crime in Gloucestershire had not declined during Gemini I, the rate of increase had slowed. The evaluation did not compare arrests or clear-ups relative to the level of crime during Gemini I with those recorded over a comparable period prior to its introduction. High profile stop and search activities appeared to transfer some of the fear of crime to offenders and, when combined with covert operations and surveillance, were believed to yield results. The publicity had been largely positive and officers believed that it had improved the public's image of the police and police morale. It was considered that the Operation would have benefited from more CID involvement or input - most Gemini officers were not trained as detectives - and from more genuinely 'covert' vehicles and additional training in covert radio procedures. A major concern was that the Gemini Units, comprising some 80 officers, had depleted the resources available for other police work.

Gemini II

On the basis of the evaluation of Gemini I, a decision was taken to re-launch Operation Gemini on an indefinite basis from 18 May 1993. The re-launch (Gemini II) was undertaken in the context of a police service undergoing significant changes: (i) a substantial re-organisation of the structure of the Constabulary whereby the original structure of two divisions, each comprising a number of sub-divisions, was replaced by five, smaller divisions with greater operational autonomy; (ii) the introduction of additional and more up-to-date information technology (IT), including a computerised and centralised crime reporting system and an integrated telephone system; and, (iii) a detailed Review of Crime Management, which reported just as Gemini II was being launched and contained a total of 64 recommendations for change, the majority of which were implemented in 1993. Most significant was the establishment of a crime management unit in each division, bringing together the collation and development of criminal intelligence and CPA, crime recording and evaluation, the allocation of cases for investigation, telephone investigation, crime prevention, crime file authorisation and the preparation of crime action plans. It is likely that these changes, which were concurrent with - and to an extent complementary to - Gemini II, contributed to the successes claimed for the operation.

There were some key differences between Gemini II and the initial, experimental operation. There was an open-ended commitment: Gemini II would continue indefinitely. Specific targets were set of a 10 percent decrease in crime and a 10 percent increase in clear-ups, though no time frame was set for the achievement of these objectives. The re-organisation of the Constabulary meant that, instead of two large Gemini Units, there were now six smaller units. The two main urban centres, Gloucester and Cheltenham, had units of 15-20 officers and the other divisions (including Cotswold division) had units of six. Gemini II was less prescriptive in that divisional commanders were empowered to set the priorities for the activities of the divisional teams. No specific budget was provided for Gemini II; costs would be met from divisional budgets.

Other important features of Gemini II were the greatly increased level of publicity, based on a defined media strategy, and the involvement of private sector sponsors. Leaflets, distributed by beat officers and through a range of other channels such as the local bus company, and specially designed posters portrayed various themes which reflected current concerns (eg. the vulnerability of property when householders are on holiday) and which were changed on a regular basis to maintain public interest. An Operation Gemini logo was brought into use on all publicity material and the name 'Gemini' was explained more precisely, both to the public and within the Constabulary. The name had been chosen to reflect the twin aims of crime prevention and detection, the dual approach combining police activity with public support, and the two types of crime - burglary and autocrime - targeted by the operation.

Most of the costs of the publicity material were met by the sponsorship of the Chelsea Building Society, a major local employer based in Cheltenham. Other firms provided assistance both in cash and in kind, such as advertising support for a crime prevention handbook and sponsorship of newspaper supplements describing the efforts of the Constabulary to deal with high volume crime.

Many of the issues raised by the evaluation of the initial operation appeared to be addressed. Some of the apparent shortcomings were dealt with by the establishment of crime management units in each of the five divisions and the new divisional structure enabled Gemini to be more widespread in its activities and brought the smaller Gemini II units closer to the ground in the rural parts of the county.

Hampshire Constabulary's strategy for dealing with burglary

Context

Hampshire comprises a mixture of urban conurbations and rural areas and has the largest population (1.5 million) of all the counties in England. Hampshire Constabulary consists of three divisions, Western, Northern and Eastern division (each comprising six or seven sub-divisions), and the Isle of Wight sub-division. The Constabulary has an establishment of some 3,269 officers and 1,196 civilian staff. Fratton sub-division, in the centre of Portsmouth, faces the usual inner city problems, including increases in house burglary and motor-vehicle crime. Winchester sub-division has a higher incidence of burglary non-dwelling than burglary dwelling. New Forest sub-division, with its wide geographical area, faces a range of problems, including burglary and 'beauty spot' crime, especially theft from cars in the summer months. The Isle of Wight has experienced an increasing number of migrant criminals, especially burglars, from the mainland and suffers from higher levels of crime, especially shoplifting, during the summer.

The Review of the Investigation of Crime and the Criminal Investigation Department

Hampshire Constabulary conducted an internal Review of the Investigation of Crime and the Criminal Investigation Department (June 1992) which identified a number of problems with the force's response to burglary and made a number of recommendations designed to provide a flexible, proactive, intelligence-based response. The proposals emphasised combating criminal offences by identifying and targeting active criminals. Those recommendations which are particularly relevant in the current context relate to:

- the restructuring of the drugs and burglary squads
- the development of an integrated intelligence system
- the adoption of crime evaluation at crime desks in every sub-division

The Review proposed that existing divisional drugs and burglary squads should be replaced by one Central Drugs and Surveillance Unit (CDSU) and three Divisional Crime and Drugs Units (DCDUs). Sub-divisions, as the basic policing units, were to continue to define and resource their own priorities, and to bid for the services of CDSU or DCDU as necessary.

It was recommended that the CDSU should come under the command of the detective chief inspector, criminal intelligence unit (CIU), and should comprise an operational team of three detective sergeants and nine detective constables, with two detective constables as Field Intelligence Officers (FIOs). In addition, six detective constables would be seconded for periods of one year to DCDUs to provide drugs expertise and intelligence support, and one detective constable would be based at CIU to deal with force drugs intelligence. The CDSU would be equipped with encrypted radio and vehicles and trained in the use of surveillance techniques.

The Review recommended that each of the three DCDUs should be commanded by a dedicated divisional detective chief inspector (operations) and should consist of an operational team of two detective sergeants and six detective constables, with one detective constable as divisional FIO and two detective constables (seconded from CDSU). Isle of Wight sub-division would retain two detective constables with responsibility for drugs matters and call on the services of Eastern DCDU when appropriate.

The proposed changes in the area of criminal intelligence were designed to improve the gathering, evaluation, development and dissemination of intelligence and to generate an effective, integrated and well-supervised intelligence system. They included changes in the structure/responsibilities of the CIU, redefinition of the role of crime analysts, and increased status, training and provision of civilian support for LIO posts.

The recommendation that each sub-division should adopt the crime desk system, with a nominated assessment officer (normally a detective sergeant) was designed to ensure that investigative resources are allocated on the basis of a professional and realistic evaluation of the seriousness of the offence, the needs of the victim and of the community, and the likelihood of detection. At times when crime desks are operational, unless an immediate response was judged to be required, all reports of crime should be directed to the crime desk for recording, evaluation and allocation. The assessment officer has a vital role in ensuring that aggrieved persons are kept informed of the progress of the investigation and in providing liaison with the press, victim support and other agencies.

The Review's recommendations were implemented from September 1992, but it should be noted that in 1992 and early 1993 some 120 CID officers were abstracted from normal duties to deal with three major murder enquiries which severely inhibited the speed of implementation. There is also local variability in implementation. In the Isle of Wight sub-division, which tries to ensure CID attendance at all domestic burglaries, CID officers operate on a three week cycle - 1: duty team; 2: back-up team; and, 3: proactive team. On New Forest sub-division, an assessment of the resource implications and success of 'screening in' all burglaries for CID attendance for an experimental period has resulted in CID attending only 'heavy' burglaries. Concerns about the centralisation of the crime units have led to the creation of sub-divisional burglary units (eg. Fratton) or ad hoc teams to undertake high profile activity in high risk areas or target active burglars (eg. Winchester).

3. Assessment: how do the three strategies compare?

Impact on burglary and other offences

Analysis of crime statistics

The first requirement of any anti-crime strategy must be that it has an impact on the targeted crime(s) - by reducing incidence or increasing the number or percentage of crimes solved, or preferably by achieving all of these outcomes. Many factors other than police resources and activity contribute to levels of crime. Economic and social changes cannot be ignored. Overall crime levels are a function of a range of complex social forces often outside the control of any policing strategy. Also, the clear-up rate is influenced by police workload, which is in turn a function of crime levels and other demands, and has questionable value as a measure of police performance (Audit Commission, 1990). However, innovative police action can have both direct and indirect effects on the number of offences committed in specific situations or contexts and is a contributory element in their detection. Therefore, if changes are seen to occur following the introduction of a new strategy, there is a *prima facie* case that the strategy has had some impact.

The available data were examined to ascertain the effects of the forces' anti-burglary strategies and the analyses presented have been selected to highlight effects on selected performance indicators.

Met-wide Bumblebee[1]

Incidence of burglary

Comparisons between the first seven-months of Met-wide Bumblebee, June to December 1993, with the same period in the previous two years, show that the decline in the recorded incidence of burglary, begun in 1992, was substantially greater in 1993 (Figure 1). In the seven months following the introduction of Met-wide Bumblebee, recorded burglary offences fell by over 14,000, a decrease of 12.8%.[2] Both burglary dwelling and burglary non-dwelling showed decreases, but the decrease was more marked for burglary dwelling (15.2%) than for non-dwelling (8.1%).

---

1   Unless otherwise stated the source for the MPD is the raw data as at January 1994.

2   Any decrease in burglary is socially significant; the observed decrease is also statistically significant (p>.01) and therefore can be judged unlikely to be due to chance variation.

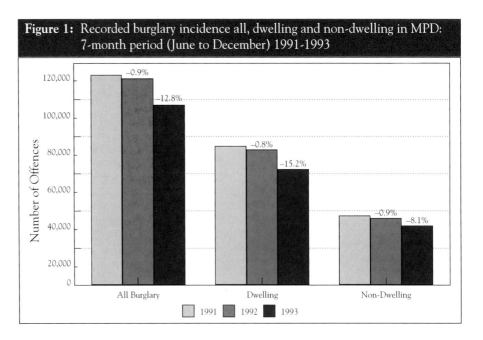

Figure 1: Recorded burglary incidence all, dwelling and non-dwelling in MPD: 7-month period (June to December) 1991-1993

Month-by-month comparisons indicate the seasonal nature of burglary - the incidence is higher during the winter months - and the impact of Bumblebee on the traditional seasonal increase. In 1993, this increase was substantially reduced and the December peak reduced by 19%, compared with 1992.

Although seven out of the eight MPD areas recorded falls in the incidence of burglary, there were both area and divisional variations in performance. On 4 Area, for example, Streatham has had more success than Croydon in halting the rising incidence of burglary both pre- and post-Bumblebee, despite facing a greater volume of burglary overall.

Detection of burglary

Over the first seven months of Met-wide Bumblebee, the clear-up rate increased for both burglary dwelling and non-dwelling, with the overall clear-up rate increasing from 10.9% in 1992 to 15% in 1993 (Figure 2).

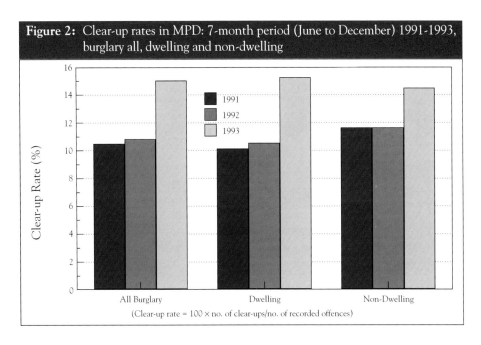

Figure 2: Clear-up rates in MPD: 7-month period (June to December) 1991-1993, burglary all, dwelling and non-dwelling

(Clear-up rate = 100 × no. of clear-ups/no. of recorded offences)

The number of clear-ups rose in 1993 for both categories of burglary offence, resulting in an 19.8% increase in the overall number of clear-ups for burglary (Table 1).

Table 1: Number of clear-ups and percentage change in number of clear-ups: MPD 7- month period (June to December) 1991-1993, burglary all, dwelling and non-dwelling.

Offence	Burglary All			Burglary Dwelling			Burglary Non-Dwelling		
Year	1991	1992	1993	1991	1992	1993	1991	1992	1993
Number of Clear-Ups	11,881	12,123	14,524	7,494	7,801	9,474	4,387	4,324	5,050
Percentage Change		+2.1	+19.8		+4.1	+21.5		-1.4	+16.8

The number of arrests showed a minimal change, but the reduction in the number of offences means that the rate of arrests per 100 offences has increased. Analyses by area show that the clear-up rate for all burglary increased in six out of the eight MPD areas, with 4 Area performing particularly well. Of the sample divisions, Holloway showed a marked improvement in performance with the clear-up rate increasing from 10.5% to 17% and the number of clear-ups increasing by 34%.

The increased clear-up rate across the MPD results from the combination of reduced incidence and the increase in the number of clear-ups. Figure 3 shows the pattern of change in the number of clear-ups for all burglary, both overall and within each of the various sub-categories of clear-up, for the seven-month period June to December, 1991 to 1993.[3]

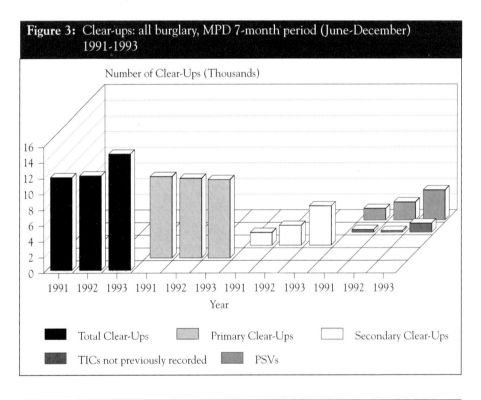

Figure 3: Clear-ups: all burglary, MPD 7-month period (June-December) 1991-1993

Number of Clear-Ups (Thousands)

Year

■ Total Clear-Ups   ▨ Primary Clear-Ups   ☐ Secondary Clear-Ups

▨ TICs not previously recorded   ▨ PSVs

---

3 i   The data on which these analyses of primary and secondary clear-ups are based were made available at a later date than the original raw data and had been revised to include clear-ups subsequently recorded. These data contain substantial increases in the number of clear-ups recorded for November and December 1993.

   ii   Clear-ups are recorded using six classifications: (1) charge or summons (ii) caution (iii) no further action (where the offender is known but there are grounds for not pursuing a prosecution) (iv) taken into consideration (TIC) where the offence was previously recorded (v) TIC where the offence was not previously recorded and (vi) post-sentence visits (PSVs) i.e. admissions to other offences secured from a convicted offender. In this report, categories (i) to (iv) are treated as primary clear-ups and categories (v) and (vi) are secondary clear-ups, in accordance with the definition used by the Audit Commission and Her Majesty's Inspectorate of Constabulary.

Although the number of clear-ups for burglary increased in 1993 compared with 1992,[4] the number of primary clear-ups fell very slightly in comparison with the previous year (-2.1%). However, it is noted that the reduction in the number of offences provides less opportunity for primary clear-ups and that the primary clear-up rate showed a small increase. In contrast with the small decline in the number of primary clear-ups, secondary clear-ups showed a dramatic increase. Over the seven-month comparison period, the number of secondary clear-ups increased by 132.3% in 1993 compared with 1992 and has nearly trebled since 1991. (The data for the twelve-month period January to December show a similar trend.)

The substantial rise in secondary clear-ups in the seven-month comparison period reflects increases in both offences taken into consideration (TICs) not previously recorded and post sentence visits (PSVs). The number of TICs not previously recorded showed a very substantial increase in 1993 compared with the previous two years and has trebled since 1991. The increase in the number of clear-ups deriving from PSVs is also marked. Over the seven-month comparison period, the number of PSVs increased by 51.8% from 1991-92 and by 89.3% from 1992-93. (Again the data for the calendar years 1991-93 show similar increases in the number of PSVs - 72.8% in 1991-92 and 113% in 1992-93.)

Figures 4a-4c show the changes in the proportion of total clear-ups for burglary which are secondary rather than primary and the changes in the proportion of secondary clear-ups which are PSVs as opposed to TICs not previously recorded. (These data refer to the seven-month comparison period but the calendar year data show a similar pattern.)

Although a greater proportion of clear-ups are primary rather than secondary, the percentage of clear-ups which are primary has declined over the past three years - from 86% in 1991, to 83% in 1992 and 67.2% in 1993. The percentage of clear-ups which are secondary has nearly doubled in the past two years, rising from 17% in 1992 to 32.8% in 1993. The percentage of secondary clear-ups which are PSVs rose to 95.7% in 1992 compared with 78.4% in 1991 but fell back to 78% in 1993.

Thus, much of the increase in the number of burglary offences solved in the first seven-months following the introduction of Met-wide Bumblebee derives from a rise in the number of secondary clear-ups, the majority of which are PSVs. One in every three burglaries solved over this period was solved by secondary means.

---

4   Analyses of the revised data for the seven-month comparison period show an increase in the number of clear-ups of 20.8% and a clear-up rate of 15.2% for burglary.

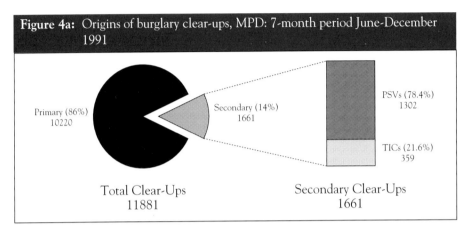

Figure 4a: Origins of burglary clear-ups, MPD: 7-month period June-December 1991

Primary (86%)
10220

Secondary (14%)
1661

PSVs (78.4%)
1302

TICs (21.6%)
359

Total Clear-Ups
11881

Secondary Clear-Ups
1661

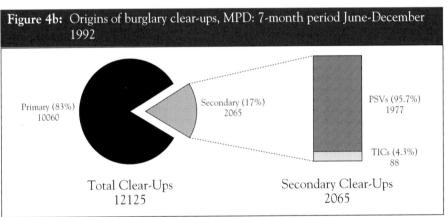

Figure 4b: Origins of burglary clear-ups, MPD: 7-month period June-December 1992

Primary (83%)
10060

Secondary (17%)
2065

PSVs (95.7%)
1977

TICs (4.3%)
88

Total Clear-Ups
12125

Secondary Clear-Ups
2065

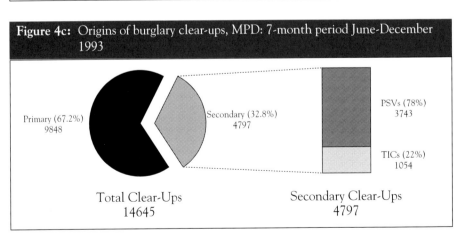

Figure 4c: Origins of burglary clear-ups, MPD: 7-month period June-December 1993

Primary (67.2%)
9848

Secondary (32.8%)
4797

PSVs (78%)
3743

TICs (22%)
1054

Total Clear-Ups
14645

Secondary Clear-Ups
4797

Other categories of offence

Since, at the time of the analysis, Bumblebee had operated Met-wide for only seven months it was difficult to determine whether displacement had occurred. It is arguable that any such operation will take time to affect criminal behaviour and therefore the crime statistics. However, analyses for the seven-month period provide little evidence to support the contention that burglars, deterred by Bumblebee, have turned to other crimes. For example, the incidence of theft and handling stolen goods (a category dominated by motor-vehicle crime) fell by 6.6% in 1993, compared with 1992. Within this category, the incidence of other theft fell and although there was an increase in theft from the person, this represents a comparatively small number of offences. Similarly, the incidence of robbery has risen slightly but not on a scale to match the reduction in burglary.

Some officers have claimed that the reduction in burglary results from changes in the way in which offences are recorded. However, the data do not provide evidence of changes in recording practice on a scale which could account in full for the decline in recorded burglaries. The incidence of criminal damage (other than to a motor vehicle) increased only marginally (1%) after the introduction of Met-wide Bumblebee. Also, the percentage of burglaries which were 'no-crimed' decreased.

Summary

Since the introduction of Met-wide Bumblebee in June 1993, the incidence of recorded burglary has fallen significantly across the MPD. The reduction is greater for burglary dwelling than for burglary non-dwelling. The number of offences solved has increased, due largely to a substantial increase in the number of secondary clear-ups, particularly PSVs. There have been increases in the clear-up rates for both burglary dwelling and burglary non-dwelling. No strong evidence was found in the crime statistics of category displacement of criminal activity or of wide-spread changes in recording practice.

Operation Gemini

Incidence of burglary

Comparisons between the first seven months of Gemini II, June to December 1993, with the same seven-month period in the previous three years, show that the recorded incidence of burglary decreased in 1993 (Figure 5). The total number of burglary offences fell by 368 in 1993, compared with 1992, a decrease of 4%. Both categories of burglary showed decreases, but the fall was greater for dwelling (-5%) than for non-dwelling (-2%). These decreases compare with substantial increases in recorded incidence in the previous two years. The decrease achieved with respect to domestic burglary is particularly noteworthy given that in the first five months of 1993 house burglaries had risen by 47% over the 1992 period.

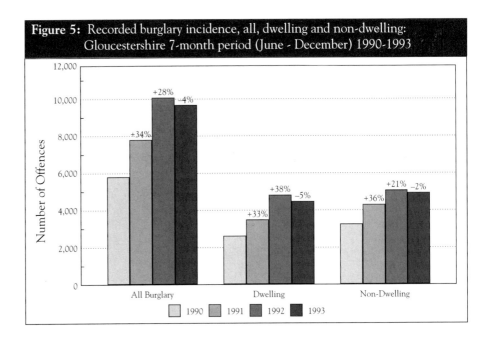

Figure 5: Recorded burglary incidence, all, dwelling and non-dwelling: Gloucestershire 7-month period (June - December) 1990-1993

When the two seven-month periods are compared, three out of the five divisions showed decreased incidence of burglary overall, with the remaining two divisions, Cotswold and Forest - both rural divisions - showing an increase (18%) and a zero percentage change, respectively.

Detection of burglary

Similar comparisons show that the clear-up rate for burglary dwelling remained static while that for burglary non-dwelling fell. The overall clear-up rate fell from 15.6% in 1992 to 13.9% in 1993 (Figure 6).

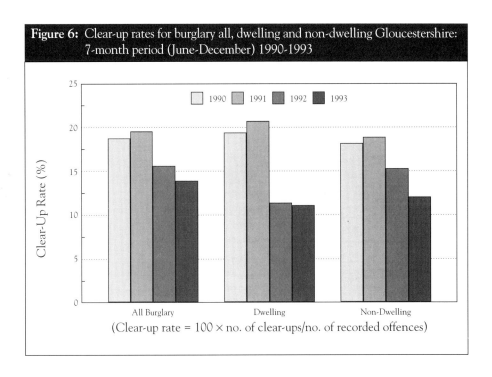

Figure 6: Clear-up rates for burglary all, dwelling and non-dwelling Gloucestershire: 7-month period (June-December) 1990-1993

(Clear-up rate = 100 × no. of clear-ups/no. of recorded offences)

The number of clear-ups fell for both categories of burglary offence, resulting in a fall of 14% in the overall number of clear-ups for burglary (Table 2). Across the five divisions, only Cheltenham division showed increases in the rate and number of clear-ups for all burglary, although Forest division showed such increases for burglary dwelling.

Table 2: Number of clear-ups and percentage change in number of clear-ups: Gloucestershire 7-month period (June to December) 1990-1993, burglary all, dwelling and non-dwelling

Offence	Burglary All				Burglary Dwelling				Burglary Non-Dwelling			
Year	1990	1991	1992	1993	1990	1991	1992	1993	1990	1991	1992	1993
Number of Clear-Ups	1,095	1,534	1,563	1,345	517	725	771	725	578	809	792	620
Percentage Change		+40	+2	−14		+40	+6	−6		+40	−2	−22

The Gloucestershire statistics initially made available did not permit an analysis of all secondary clear-ups, since the only sub-category of detections referred to those arising from prison visits. However, these data provided no evidence of any dramatic increase in the number or percentage of prison visit clear-ups associated with the introduction of Operation Gemini. The number and percentage of clear-ups which resulted from prison visits did increase in 1992 and again in 1993 for burglary dwelling but generally declined for burglary non-dwelling. For all burglary, the number of clear-ups resulting from prison visits fell, but since the total number of detections also declined, this results in a small rise in the percentage of detections which derive from prison visits - from 38% in 1992 to 42% in 1993. The number of visits to offenders with non-custodial sentences is known to be extremely small and therefore does not contribute significantly to the number of secondary detections. Data obtained subsequently for the calendar years 1991-93, which do permit a more detailed analysis, indicate that the percentage of detections for burglary achieved by secondary means has remained static over the three-year period at 43-45% (Home Office, 1994). Although the percentage of secondary detections which are PSVs rose from 84.8% in 1991 to 91.6% in 1992, it was virtually unchanged in 1993 (91.3%).

Motor-vehicle crime

Similar comparisons between the first seven months of Gemini II, June to December 1993, with the same seven-month period in the previous three years, show that the recorded incidence of motor-vehicle crime increased in 1993 but the percentage increase was lower than that recorded in 1991 and 1992. The total number of motor-vehicle offences increased by 280 in 1993, compared with 1992, an increase of 3%. There was no change in the incidence of theft from a motor vehicle (compared with a 22% increase in 1992) and an increase of 11% in the incidence of theft of a motor vehicle/TWOC (compared with a zero percentage change in 1992). Over the seven-month period, two divisions, Gloucester and Cheltenham - both primarily urban locations - recorded decreases in the overall incidence of motor-vehicle crime. The other divisions showed increased incidence, ranging from 15-16% in Stroud and Forest to 69% in Cotswold division.

The number of clear-ups and the clear-up rates for motor-vehicle crime fell over the seven-month period following the introduction of Gemini II. Overall, clear-ups decreased by 26% and the clear-up rate fell from 11.9% in 1992 to 8.5% in 1993. The greater fall in clear-up rate observed for theft of a motor vehicle/TWOC, compared with theft from a motor vehicle, is due to the combination of a smaller number of clear-ups and increased incidence for this category of offence.

Summary

Following the introduction of Gemini II and the implementation of other changes in the management of crime, at a time when burglary had increased dramatically, the incidence of burglary has shown a small percentage decrease across the force. However, decreased incidence is restricted to those divisions which are urban, rather than rural, in nature.

Operation Gemini is also aimed at motor-vehicle crime and here the percentage increase across the force slowed in 1993 compared with the immediately preceding two years. Again, the effect is restricted to primarily urban divisions. The increases in burglary and motor-vehicle crime, particularly on Cotswold division - the most rural of the five divisions - could indicate some displacement of criminal activity.

The changes in the number of clear-ups and in clear-up rates, for burglary and motor-vehicle crime do vary across divisions. However, the falls in both clear-up numbers and rates across the force, for both types of offence, show that overall detection performance has not yet improved since the introduction of Gemini II.

Hampshire's approach[5]

Incidence of burglary

In the first year following implementation of the Review, September to August 1992/93, the incidence of burglary rose by 6.7%, compared with the previous year. However, calendar year comparisons show a year-on-year decrease of 4.3% in 1993, compared with an increase (7.9%) in the previous year (Figure 7).

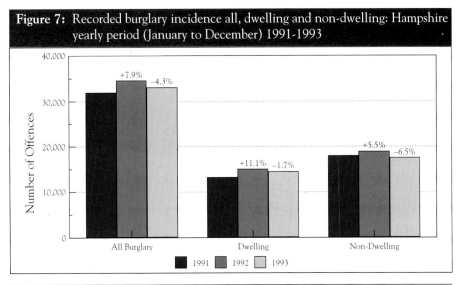

Figure 7: Recorded burglary incidence all, dwelling and non-dwelling: Hampshire yearly period (January to December) 1991-1993

5   The recommendations of the Review were implemented in September 1992. Comparisons were carried out for three different time periods: (i) September to August, 1991/92 vs. 1992/93; (ii) calendar years 1991-3 and, (iii) September to December, 1991-93.

The fall in 1993 was greater for burglary non-dwelling (6.5%), than for burglary dwelling (1.7%). Decreases in burglary non-dwelling were evident in two out of the three divisions, Western (9.1%) and Eastern (11.2%), and in the Isle of Wight sub-division (1.8%). Decreases in burglary dwelling were restricted to Western division (4.1%) and the Isle of Wight sub-division (32.4%).

The 1992/93 comparisons suggest that the changes arising from the Review were slow to take effect and any impact they may have had was not evident until 1993. Comparisons for the four-month period, September to December, confirm this interpretation. Whereas burglary increased in the last four months of 1992, compared with the previous year, it decreased in the same period in 1993, by 22.3% for domestic burglary and 13.9% for non-dwelling burglary - an overall reduction of 18%.

Detection of burglary

In the year following the implementation of the Review's recommendations in September 1992, the clear-up rate for burglary fell, from 18.6% in 1991/92 to 15.9% in 1992/93, and the number of detections for burglary decreased by 8.6%.

Comparisons based on calendar years show that the clear-up rate for burglary fell from 19.5% in 1991 to 16.1% in 1992, but remained static in 1993 (Figure 8).

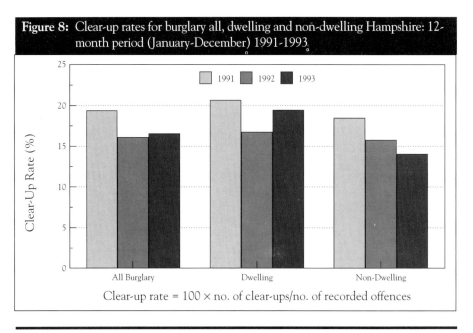

Figure 8: Clear-up rates for burglary all, dwelling and non-dwelling Hampshire: 12-month period (January-December) 1991-1993

Clear-up rate = 100 × no. of clear-ups/no. of recorded offences

Calendar year comparisons also show that the number of clear-ups for burglary fell in both 1992 and 1993, compared with the previous year (Table 3). However, the decline was smaller in 1993 (2.9%) than in 1992 (10%). Also, there was an increase in the detection rate for domestic burglary which results from the combination of decreased incidence and an increase in the number of clear-ups. The number of clear-ups for domestic burglary in that year rose by 12.3%, compared with a decline (8.6%) in the previous year, with two of the three divisions (Northern and Western) showing increases. These analyses, together with the four-month comparisons, suggest that there has been some improvement in the number of domestic burglary offences solved but that this improvement has taken some time to emerge.

Table 3: Number of clear-ups and percentage change in number of clear-ups: Hampshire 12-month period (January to December) 1991-1993, burglary all, dwelling and non-dwelling

Offence	Burglary All			Burglary Dwelling			Burglary Non-Dwelling		
Year	1991	1992	1993	1991	1992	1993	1991	1992	1993
Number of Clear-Ups	6,245	5,623	5,458	2,903	2,654	2,981	3,342	2,969	2,477
Percentage Change		–10	–2.9		–8.6	+12.3		–11.2	–16.6

An examination of secondary clear-ups recorded by Hampshire Constabulary[6] (for calendar years and for the four-month comparison period) shows little evidence of any consistent trend since the implementation of the CID recommendations. For example, calendar year comparisons show that the percentage of clear-ups for burglary which are secondary rose from 25.8% in 1991 to 28.3% in 1992 but fell back to 23.2% in 1993. The number of secondary clear-ups for burglary showed a minimal decrease in 1992 compared with the previous year but fell by 20.5% in 1993 compared with 1992, reflecting falls both in the number of TICs not previously recorded and in the number of PSVs. The percentage of secondary clear-ups which are PSVs shows minimal variation over the three-year period, ranging from 78.5% in 1992 to 81.7% in 1993. Analyses for burglary dwelling and non-dwelling reveal a similar picture but again there is no consistent discernible trend. Thus, calendar year comparisons do not show any increase in the number or percentage of

---

6   The data on which the analyses of primary and secondary clear-ups are based were made available at a later date than the original data and have been revised to include clear-ups subsequently recorded.

secondary clear-ups or any change in their composition. Over the past three years, one in four detections was achieved by secondary means and of these four out five were PSVs.

<u>Motor-vehicle crime</u>

In the year following the implementation of the Review, the incidence of motor-vehicle crime (theft of, from and TWOC) rose marginally (1.9%) over the previous year. Calendar year comparisons show a decreased incidence in 1993 (3.8%), compared with a rise in 1992 (3.1%). Again, this suggests that the changes resulting from the Review have been slow to take effect. Comparisons for the four-month period show a decrease of 12.7% in the incidence of motor-vehicle crime in 1993, compared with a rise of 4% in 1992.

All of the comparisons for the number of detections for motor-vehicle offences show a year-on-year decrease. The comparisons of clear-up rates show a similar picture. The clear-up rate for motor-vehicle crime decreased in the year immediately following the Review, and declined in 1993, after having been static in 1991 and 1992. The four-month comparisons also show a decline, although that observed in 1993 is less than in the previous year.

<u>Summary</u>

There is little evidence of an immediate impact of the implementation of the Review's recommendations on the incidence and detection of burglary and motor-vehicle crime. However, there is evidence that the changes implemented from September 1992 are beginning to take effect. In 1993, the incidence of burglary declined and the number of detections and the detection rate for domestic burglary increased. These changes were particularly evident in the latter part of the year. Motor-vehicle crime also showed a decline in 1993, especially in the last four months, but the number and percentage of offences solved show no improvements over the previous year.

Comparison across the three forces

Whereas Met-wide Bumblebee and Operation Gemini had similar starting dates, in mid-May/June 1993, the changes in Hampshire were implemented over a period from September 1992. In order to make comparisons across the three forces, the same seven-month period (June to December) was taken for both the MPS and Gloucestershire, while the data for Hampshire refer to full calendar years. The choice of this time period reflects the fact that the changes in Hampshire do not relate to a defined strategy, with a specific launch date, as was the case with both Bumblebee and Gemini, and have taken some time to be implemented.

The comparison data for recorded incidence of burglary (Figure 9) show that, although the incidence of burglary declines in all three forces, the percentage decline following the introduction of Bumblebee was three-times the magnitude of the decreases observed in both Gloucestershire and Hampshire.

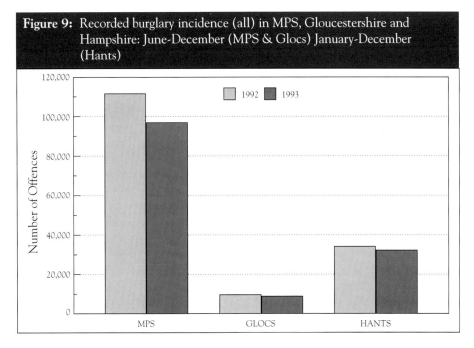

Figure 9: Recorded burglary incidence (all) in MPS, Gloucestershire and Hampshire: June-December (MPS & Glocs) January-December (Hants)

The MPS is the only one of the three forces to show increases in both the number and percentage of burglary offences solved (Table 4). However, the increase in detections in this case derives to a large extent from secondary clear-ups.

Table 4: Clear-up rate (%) and number of clear-ups for burglary (all) in MPS, Gloucestershire and Hampshire: June to December (MPS & Glocs), January to December (Hants)

	MPS		Gloucestershire		Hampshire	
Year	1992	1993	1992	1993	1992	1993
Clear-Up Rate %	10.9	15	15.6	13.9	16.1	16.5
Number of Clear-Ups	12,125	14,524	1,563	1,345	5,623	5,458

Overview

Impact on burglary: the research period

In the first seven months following the introduction of Met-wide Bumblebee, the MPS saw a substantial reduction in the incidence of burglary and achieved increases in both the number of offences cleared-up and the clear-up rate for burglary. These improvements in performance are greater than those achieved in the two comparison forces over the time periods encompassed by the research and they suggest that the high profile, proactive approach embodied in Bumblebee has had an impact. However, there are a number of points which should be noted.

It is not possible to establish with certainty a causal link between police activity and changes in the incidence of recorded crime. Many factors will affect the level of crime, not least the social and economic climate at the time. It is interesting that reductions in burglary across the MPD - although not of the magnitude associated with Bumblebee - were also recorded in 1987 and 1988, a period of general economic recovery. Also, in England and Wales there has been a fall in the number of recorded burglaries of 4.2% in the period June to December 1993 compared with the same seven-month period in 1992. A similar comparison for the Metropolitan forces other than the MPS (i.e. Greater Manchester, City of London, Merseyside, Northumbria, South Yorkshire, West Midlands and West Yorkshire) shows a 3% reduction in the number of recorded burglaries. Among the forty police forces in England and Wales not involved in the evaluation, seven have registered decreases of 10% or more in the number of recorded burglaries and five forces - Avon and Somerset, City of London, Cumbria, Sussex and Gwent - show reductions in excess of that registered by the MPS. Of these five forces, both Avon and Somerset and Sussex have high profile anti-burglary operations and the City of London Force has introduced anti-terrorist measures which are likely to have affected the incidence of burglary.

Incidence levels will also be affected by recording practices. Although no clear-cut evidence was found to support the contention that the MPS figures for the incidence of burglary have been improved by the reclassification of some burglary offences - for example as criminal damage or theft - or by no-criming offences, it would be naive to assume that there are no variations in recording practice. However, examination of the crime statistics indicated that, while reclassification may occur in certain cases, this practice could not have been sufficient by itself to account for the fall in recorded burglary.

A substantial proportion of the increase in detections for burglary offences across the MPD is accounted for by the increase in secondary detections. Since the introduction of Met-wide Bumblebee the proportion of clear-ups for burglary which are secondary detections has doubled, with the result that in the first seven months of the Operation (June - December 1993) one in every three burglary offences solved were secondary detections. This increased proportion is higher than that observed in Hampshire, where one in every four burglaries solved were secondary detections but lower than that in Gloucestershire where over four out of ten detections for burglary are achieved by secondary means. However, in contrast with the MPS, the proportion of clear-ups which are secondary has remained relatively stable in both Hampshire and Gloucestershire over the past three years.

As pointed out earlier, the increase in secondary detections achieved by the MPS reflects increases both in the number of TICs not previously recorded and in the number of PSVs. (The composition of the secondary detections for burglary is broadly comparable across the three forces, with between eight out of ten (MPS and Hampshire Constabulary) and nine out of ten (Gloucestershire Constabulary) secondary detections for burglary being attributable to PSVs in 1993.) There are a number of different factors which might contribute to the increase in the number of TICs not previously recorded and PSVs within the MPD. These include greater management emphasis on improved detection rates, more skilled interviewing techniques and the allocation of resources necessary to substantiate admitted offences.

One explanation for the increase in the number of PSVs is that the MPS is putting more effort into interviewing convicted offenders not only with custodial but also with non-custodial sentences. This is clearly a key element in the MPS strategy. Another explanation is that there has been a qualitative shift in the population of those arrested for burglary, with more arrests of prolific offenders who have more offences to admit to - either as TICs or PSVs. This could also account for the lack of increase in the number of arrests, since resources are directed toward 'quality' arrests rather than quantity. Again this is part of the MPS's approach, but this explanation does raise questions about the implications of clearing-up these offences as PSVs. Clearly it is advantageous to criminals to admit to other offences after they have been sentenced, rather than asking for them to be taken into consideration in court. On the other hand, it may be helpful for victims to be informed that the identity of the offender is known. The guidance provided by Her Majesty's Inspectorate of Constabulary (HMIC) on how to dispose of crimes detected from prison visits does in fact state that the views of the complainant should be sought when deciding how to dispose of such detections (HMIC, 1987).

However, whether an increasing emphasis on PSVs, which are likely to result in no further action against offenders, is in the long-term interests of anti-crime strategies and of the public will continue to be the subject of debate.

When Gemini was introduced in Gloucestershire, the Constabulary was facing substantial year-on-year increases in burglary. The fact that Gemini II has been associated with a decline in the incidence of burglary, but that this decline has been less than that associated with Bumblebee, may partly reflect the scale of the problem the Constabulary was encountering at the time the operation was introduced. Also, the effect of Gemini has been greater in the urban than in the rural areas of the county, which will have affected the Operation's success across the county as a whole. The statistical data for the period up to December 1993 indicate that the operation has not yet had a significant impact on the number of burglary offences detected or the detection rate. However, the substantial increase in secondary detections evident in the MPS is not a feature associated with Gemini. Overall, the early evidence is encouraging and indicates that Operation Gemini is worthy of further development.

In Hampshire, where strategy is not directed specifically toward burglary and lacks a publicised 'brand name', there is also some evidence that changes in approach are now beginning to have an impact. It is likely that initial attempts to implement a more proactive approach to crime were hampered by abstractions for major enquiries, but there is now evidence of reduced incidence of burglary. There has also been some improvement in the number of domestic burglary offences solved and, as in Gloucestershire, there is no evidence of a dramatic increase in the number of secondary detections.

Displacement

A targeted strategy carries with it the risk of displacement, either to other categories of crime or to different geographical locations, and this needs to be monitored. There is little evidence of displacement to other crimes in the MPD, although it is possible that some of the increase in theft from the person and in robbery may be attributable to diversification by burglars. There is some suggestion that displacement of criminal activity may have occurred in Gloucestershire, either geographical or category displacement, or a combination of the two.

Other categories of crime

Preliminary evidence from the MPS and Gloucestershire suggests that focusing attention on burglary can yield welcome results in respect of other crimes, particularly drug offences, since a substantial proportion of offenders are also drug users and/or dealers.

Impact on burglary: up-date[7]

The latest available crime statistics, which cover the period July 1993 to June 1994, confirm that many police forces in England and Wales have recorded a fall in the number of burglary offences (Home Office, 1994). Across England and Wales there was an 8% fall in the number of recorded burglaries, compared with increases of 9% in the twelve months to June 1993 and 16% in the twelve months to June 1992. Over the twelve-month period to June 1994, the falls in number of burglary offences recorded by the MPS (−14%) and by Gloucestershire (−3%) are comparable to those relating to the research period. Thus the MPS and Gloucestershire Constabulary appear to be sustaining the reduction in burglary offences associated with the introduction of their respective operations. In the case of Gloucestershire Constabulary, there is also some preliminary evidence of a further fall in the number of recorded burglaries. Comparisons for the nine-month period January to September show that domestic burglary fell by 6% and other burglaries by 5% in 1994, compared with 1993. There is also evidence of a reduction in burglary in some of the rural divisions. Over the same twelve-month period July 1993 to June 1994, Hampshire Constabulary recorded a fall in burglary offences of 14%, which is substantially greater than that which was evident in the twelve-month period following the implementation of the Review or in the calendar year 1993, and is identical with that achieved within the MPS. This fall in the incidence of burglary in Hampshire between July 1993 and June 1994 is congruent with the view expressed earlier that Hampshire's crime strategy had been hampered in the early stages of its implementation but was beginning to have an impact.

The decreases in the number of burglary offences recorded by the three comparison forces during the twelve months to June 1994 must be seen in the context of the changes in burglary incidence recorded elsewhere in England and Wales. Of the forty forces not involved in this study, thirty-two have registered percentage decreases in burglary, seventeen have registered decreases of 10% or more in the number of recorded burglary offences and nine forces - Avon and Somerset, Cambridgeshire, Cumbria, City of London, Norfolk, Surrey, Sussex, Dyfed-Powys and North Wales - show reductions equal to or greater than the 14% fall registered by both the MPS and Hampshire. Although several of these forces have taken special steps to counter burglary and the figures take no account of the scale of the problem facing individual forces in the preceding year, the number of forces recording decreases in burglary and the magnitude of those decreases reinforce the view that the reduction in burglary incidence associated with the strategies under

---

7   The research report on which this published version is based was submitted in May 1994. New information has become available during the period of the review process and preparation for publication.

consideration are multiply-determined, reflecting both strategy implementation and exogenous factors.

Concerns that decreases in the number of recorded burglary offences may be due, at least in part, to changes in the likelihood of victims reporting such offences and/or by changes in police recording practices have been highlighted by the publication of the initial findings from the 1994 British Crime Survey (BCS) (Mayhew *et al*, 1994). Comparisons between the BCS data for 1994 and for 1992 (Mayhew *et al*, 1992) suggest that there may have been a decrease both in the percentage of crimes reported to the police and in the percentage of reported offences which were recorded by the police. The BCS is a household survey and as such is prone to certain forms of error. It also necessarily excludes crimes against businesses. Therefore, the BCS data and comparative police figures for burglary refer to domestic burglary only. However, they do suggest that, although burglaries - especially those involving loss - are more likely to be reported than some other categories of crime, the percentage of burglaries which are reported has fallen by 4% (from 73% in 1991 to 69% in 1993). The data also suggest that the percentage of reported burglaries which are recorded by the police has fallen by 3% (from 63% in 1992 to 60% in 1994). Victims appear not to report crimes mainly because they feel that they are not serious enough or that the police will not be able to take effective action. In the case of burglary, a reduction in the readiness to report offences may be related to insurance cover. In high-risk areas, such as inner cities, there has been a small decline in insurance cover and there has also been a drop in claims made by insured victims. The drop in claims may reflect changes in the conditions of the insurance policies, such as acceptance of a higher level of 'excess' to minimise premiums or more stringent conditions on coverage, the desire to protect no-claims bonuses or to avoid an increase in premiums in the future.

Decreases in the proportion of burglary offences which are reported and in the proportion of reported offences which are subsequently recorded by the police could, either alone or in combination, contribute to the observed fall in the recorded incidence of burglary. However, there are no data sources, apart from the BCS, which make it possible to verify the contention that either of these factors do play a major role in the reduction in burglary. If the police are not recording a higher proportion of reported burglaries, then it is likely that these would be attempted burglaries or burglaries with no loss. However, this practice would have to be routine and widespread in order to make a significant contribution to the substantial decreases in burglary which have been observed in some forces (including the MPS and Hampshire) in the twelve-month period to June 1994.

Similarly, changes in the way in which some burglaries are classified could contribute to a fall in the number of recorded burglaries. However, comparing the twelve months to June 1994 with the previous twelve months reveals a negligible percentage change (less than one percent) in the incidence of criminal damage within the MPS and only a small increase (2%) in criminal damage offences recorded in Hampshire. In the third force, Gloucestershire, criminal damage has increased (by 24%) but Gloucestershire is the force which shows the smallest decline in burglary (–3%), while one might expect the reverse to be true if some burglaries were being classified as criminal damage.

Obviously, any or all of these factors - changes in the likelihood of reporting, non-recording or re-classification of burglary offences - may contribute to some degree to the observed decline in recorded burglaries in any of the three comparison forces. However, the BCS data relating to reporting behaviour by the public and police non-recording are suggestive rather than conclusive. Neither is there any strong evidence that a substantial proportion of burglary offences are being classified as criminal damage. Moreover, none of these factors on its own could account for a decrease of the magnitude recorded by the MPS and, more recently, by Hampshire.

The clear-up rate for burglary within the MPS for the twelve-month period August 1993 to July 1994 was 17.6%, compared with 12.3% for the same period in 1992-93. Thus, the MPS appears to be maintaining the improvement in its detection rate for burglary offences. The increased reliance on secondary clear-ups has continued. Comparisons for the twelve-month period August 1993 to July 1994 with the same period for 1992-93 show that while the number of primary clear-ups has declined by 5%, the number of secondary clear-ups has increased by 103.8%. Over this twelve-month period to July 1994, the percentage of clear-ups which were secondary rather than primary was 42.2% compared with 25.4% over the same period in 1992-93. In the first seven months of 1994, the percentage of clear-ups which were secondary rose to 46.4%. Thus, just under half the burglaries solved in the second seven months of Met-wide Bumblebee were solved by secondary means, compared with a third in the first seven months of the operation.

In the first nine months of 1994, the number of detections for burglary in Gloucestershire increased by 8%, with primary detections showing an increase of 23%. Reliance on secondary detections decreased, with secondary detections comprising 34.7% of all detections for burglary in the first nine months of 1994, compared with 42.4% during the same period in 1993. In Hampshire, detections for burglary fell by 5.4% compared with the same period in 1993 and there is some preliminary evidence of an increased reliance on secondary detections for burglary over this nine-month period, compared with the same period in 1993. The number of primary detections for burglary decreased by 17.7% while the number of secondary detections increased by 36.2%, reflecting increases both in the number of TICs not previously recorded (+12.1%) and in the number of PSVs (+42.1%). The percentage of all clear-ups for burglary which were achieved by secondary means increased from 22.7% in the first nine months of 1993 to 32.7% in the first nine months of 1994. Thus, a third of all detections for burglary in Hampshire during the period January to September 1994 were achieved by secondary means.

These supplementary data highlight the problems associated with evaluating the impact of anti-crime strategies using the recorded incidence of a targeted crime and clear-ups as performance indicators. However, they do indicate that, while all three forces have continued to experience a reduction in recorded burglary, the reduction in Hampshire is now comparable with that which exists across the MPD. In Gloucestershire, the magnitude of the reduction in burglary incidence, although smaller than in the other two forces, has increased in recent months. In contrast with the other two forces, the number of secondary detections for burglary has decreased in Gloucestershire and the recent increase in the number of burglary detections arises from an increase in the number of primary detections. Within the MPD and, more recently in Hampshire, there is evidence of an increase in the number of detections for burglary which are achieved by secondary means. This increase in secondary detections is accompanied by a reduction in the number of primary detections for burglary and, in the case of the MPS, is the reason for the improvement in the overall number of detections for burglary across the MPD.

Recording practice: recent MPS guidance

The MPS has recently published a booklet offering guidance to officers concerning the recording of crime and clear-ups (Metropolitan Police, 1994). The booklet outlines good practice for investigators, some of which is new, and is allied to a similar booklet for local managers which was published earlier in the year. It is emphasised that integrity is paramount in recording practice and is not incompatible with effectiveness. At the same time it is pointed out that, from a victim's perspective, a solved crime - by whatever means - matters.

The booklet gives advice about all stages of the investigative process and associated recording practice and makes some specific references to burglary. For example, burglary offences are identified as frequently difficult to classify and there is simple guidance given concerning the classification of residential and non-residential burglary and the distinction between offences of attempted burglary and criminal damage. The importance of solving crime, not only to provide a service to the victim by identifying the person responsible, but also to improve the force's detection rate and prevent the loss of valuable intelligence is highlighted at the beginning of the sections outlining good practice in identifying TICs and PSVs. Officers are advised that they should adopt a deliberate practice of questioning all offenders they interview to discover other offences they have committed, especially where property is involved, for example, burglary or fraud. Guidance is provided as to the conditions under which authorisation may be given for interviews with serving prisoners and the appropriate steps to be taken. Some divisions have appointed a dedicated post-sentence visits officer, while others rely on individual officers. It is stated that, while in the past post-sentence interviews have, in the main, been confined to those in prison, there is no reason why investigators should not make contact with and interview convicted people who receive a non-custodial sentence, using the same criteria as those which apply to prison interviews.

Police perspectives and level of support

Burglary: priority, prevention and detection

Officers are unlikely to give their full support to an anti-crime strategy unless they see the targeted crime(s) as a problem and they consider the strategy to be an effective response. The interviews with officers showed that the majority saw burglary as having a high priority on the agendas of both police and public. Burglary was identified as the major crime-related problem facing the police by all three forces and was seen as giving rise to most public concern by two out of the three forces. Motor-vehicle crime, drug-related crime and street crime/robberies were also regarded as major problems, with motor-vehicle crime being seen as the primary source of public concern in Gloucestershire.

Overall, burglary was identified as the most important problem facing the police and the public because of its prevalence, intrusive nature and the traumatic effects on victims. However, drugs were regarded as the most important issue by a minority of officers (mainly in urban areas), who saw drugs (especially crack cocaine) as the primary cause of a range of offences. For example, on Holloway division, in December 1993, eight of the ten most active burglars were crack cocaine addicts and the remaining two were addicted to heroin.

Senior officers in all three forces placed emphasis on targeting known criminals, more effective use of criminal intelligence and CPA, a high standard of investigation, sympathetic victim support and crime prevention. The majority felt that they were making progress but were constrained by the shortage of human resources and equipment, such as IT, encrypted radios and covert vehicles. There was general concern about the investigative skills of officers and the need for additional training for first officers at scenes of crime. The importance of raising public awareness of the need to protect their property and engaging in proactive policing was confirmed by their emergence as the most important police actions to combat burglary (Table 5). The public's major responsibilities were seen to be protecting and marking their property and increased co-operation with the police.

Officers had clear ideas about what the public was entitled to expect of them in relation to burglary: a prompt response; a professional, efficient but sympathetic approach; the provision of information to victims (including contact with Victim

Table 5: Officers' views: most important actions by police and public to combat burglary		
	Police actions	Public actions
Prevent burglary	Raise public awareness of need to protect own property (eg. securing/ listing/marking)	Protect/mark own property
	Arrest known/persistent burglars	Vigilance/inform police re. anything suspicious
	High profile policing on the streets	Active Neighbourhood Watch (Hampshire)
Detect burglary	Proactive policing/targeting of known criminals/increased use of criminal intelligence and CPA	Vigilance/increased willingness to inform police of suspicious behaviour (police must educate public re. their role)
	Direct resources into burglary (eg. specialist squads)	Identify/photograph/mark property
	Better standard of investigation (especially by first officer at scene) and more SOCOs	Support Neighbourhood Watch (MPS)
	Increased use of post-sentence visits (Hants)	
	Support for victims and witnesses	

Support); and, an honest account of investigative progress and likelihood of success. A majority felt that they met public expectations given the limited resources. Criticisms focused on inadequate investigation - especially by the first officer at the scene - duplication of effort and lack of follow-up information to victims.

While some officers argued that all burglaries should be 'screened in' for investigation, the majority felt that, where there was little on which to base an investigation, lack of resources made it difficult to justify a full investigation. Also, although most officers equated a prompt response with attendance at the scene, a significant number argued that, unless the burglar had been disturbed or the victim was elderly, otherwise vulnerable or extremely distressed, it was appropriate to delay attendance or even deal with the report by telephone (cf. Helping with Enquiries. Audit Commission, 1993).

Aspects of current organisation and practice

<u>Perceived changes</u>

Operation Bumblebee: Most officers detected some differences between Operation Bumblebee and the MPS's previous approach to burglary. A minority regarded Bumblebee merely as a restatement of former practice or, as one officer (1 Area) put it: 'We are not doing anything different, we are just doing it differently'. On the positive side, officers noted the higher public profile for burglary and the existence of a formal strategy for its investigation - rather than merely recording reported offences - based on increased proactivity and supported by the creation of dedicated area and divisional squads and other resource allocation. Bumblebee had also resulted in more crime prevention initiatives and an improved quality of service to victims.

On the negative side, there were concerns about the loss of officers to the Bumblebee squads, the impact of Bumblebee on the investigation of other crimes and the range of experience gained by junior officers. Officers questioned the prescriptive nature of Bumblebee, arguing, for example, that the requirement to 'screen in' all residential burglaries for investigation was neither efficient nor viable. There were allegations that senior officers were 'cooking the books' to make the operation look successful but no evidence was presented to support this assertion. The increasing emphasis on PSVs, especially to those with non-custodial sentences, which was seen to be associated with Operation Bumblebee, was also the source of some concern.

Operation Gemini: In Gloucestershire, most officers noted differences between Gemini and the previous approach to burglary and vehicle-related crime. The major organisational change noted was the establishment of specialist Gemini units, about which officers had mixed views. For every officer who endorsed the creation of the dedicated teams, there was one who was concerned that the teams had depleted the strength of the regular shifts or had left the CID shorthanded.

Other organisational changes noted were the establishment of crime management units and strengthening of intelligence units. Although these changes resulted from the review of crime management, they were perceived as part of, or as attributable to, Operation Gemini. Other differences associated with Gemini were the better use of criminal intelligence and CPA, a move from a reactive to a proactive approach, an increase in the level of publicity and an increased workload.

Hampshire's approach: The primary outcome of the Review was seen to be the establishment of crime desks and the associated posts of crime manager and assessment officer, resulting in the appropriate allocation of resources and a streamlining of procedures. Depending on the nature of the crime report and the pressure on resources, the assessment officer 'puts away', refers the crime back to the uniformed officer who conducted the initial investigation for follow-up action or allocates it to CID for further enquiries. The changes arising from the introduction of crime desks, though not without criticism, were generally agreed to be an effective use of personnel, to have increased proactivity and to have improved the service provided to the public in general and burglary victims in particular.

The establishment of the CDSU and the DCDUs were also identified as major innovations resulting from the implementation of the Review. The focus of these units on proactive work, based on improved intelligence and targeting of criminals, was endorsed by the majority. The introduction of FIOs and LIOs with a more proactive role was welcomed. However, despite these changes, activity was not generally seen to be intelligence-led. There was criticism of the force's capacity to record, analyse and disseminate both criminal intelligence and crime information. The lack of appropriate IT and trained personnel - especially for surveillance - often resulted in a reactive rather than a proactive approach. It was also argued that the lack of a dedicated burglary squad and the pooling of personnel in a multi-purpose DCDU resulted in the balance of activity being shifted in favour of drugs, at the expense of burglary.

Preparation for change: Although the majority of officers had neither received nor felt the need for any special training to prepare them for changes in their force's approach to burglary, a significant minority would have welcomed additional training in a range of areas, but especially in surveillance.

Commonalities across forces

A set of fifteen actions or procedures, selected from those required or recommended for Met-wide Bumblebee, was used to compare practice across the three forces (Table 6). The MPD areas are detailed separately because of their variability. The pattern of responses (from senior officers) indicates that there is some similarity in practice, especially between the MPS and Gloucestershire.

Table 6: Elements of current strategy: frequency of occurrence in the three forces ('All', 'Most' and 'None' refer to the proportion of respondents who stated that a named action is taken)

	Element	MPS			Glocs	Hants
		1 Area	4 Area	2, 5 & 7 Area		
a.	Explanatory information/presentations (re. problem of burglary) to local opinion makers/committees, CPS, Magistrates, Judges, Neighbourhood Watch, etc	All	Most	Most	All	All
b.	Information about your burglary strategy/success provided to local press	All	All	All	All	Most
c.	Crime Prevention Officers targeted towards burglary	All	All	All	All	All
d.	Informants told priority given to arrests for burglary/recovery of stolen property	Most	All	All	Some	Some
e.	Surveillance teams directed towards burglary	Most	All	Most	Some	Some
f.	Beat/sector officers given 'targets' for regular intelligence (eg. adopt a burglar)	Some	Most	Most	All	Some
g.	Statements of burglary victims to include information re. level of trauma suffered	Some	Some	All	Some	Some
h.	Following arrest, each burglar's address searched (within PACE)	All	All	All	All	All
i.	All officers reminded of responsibilities as first officer at scene of crime, through training days	All	All	All	Most	Some
j.	High profile search and arrest operations carried out	All	All	All	Most	Some
k.	All officers given basic crime prevention training	All	All	All	All	Some
l.	All property coming into police possession examined by ultra-violet lamp for identification marks	Most	Most	All	Most	Most
m.	When suspects' premises searched, property examined with ultra-violet lamps for markings and to promote belief large amounts of property are marked	Some	All	Some	Some	Some
n.	Districts prone to high incidence of burglary targeted for crime prevention work (eg. with 'burglary free' days)	Most	All	Most	Some	Some
o.	Post-sentence visits to people with non-custodial sentences for burglary offences	Some	Some	Most	Some	None

Some contentious issues

Post-sentence visits: Operation Bumblebee encourages PSVs to offenders with both custodial and non-custodial sentences. It is argued that the victims of burglary ideally want offenders caught and convicted, and their property recovered but, failing that, they would like to know that the identity of the offender is known to the police. The counter argument is that post-sentence clear-ups are complex and time-consuming and therefore PSVs are a diversion of resources. Many MPS officers actively oppose PSVs to offenders with non-custodial sentences, arguing that they are immoral and that it is not within their power to grant an 'amnesty' to offenders who admit other, more serious offences. Disquiet about the legitimacy of PSVs to those with non-custodial sentences was also expressed by officers in Gloucestershire and in Hampshire. Both Operation Gemini and Hampshire's strategy encourage PSVs to offenders with custodial sentences only. Hampshire Constabulary expressly forbids PSVs to offenders with non-custodial sentences.

Victim impact statements: Support for victim impact statements is not universal. There is some concern that advising courts of the effects on a victim of a criminal offence, such as burglary - including any physical, financial, social or psychological harm - may be counterproductive. One major source of concern is that the information contained in the victim impact statement may be challenged by defence lawyers, resulting in victims being cross-examined about the validity of their claims. It is also argued that the perceived impact depends on the resilience of the victim and, in cases where victims cope well with the aftermath of an offence, this could result in a lighter sentence. Such misgivings are shared by some of those involved in Victim Support (cf. The National Conference of Victim Support, 1993).

High profile search and arrest operations: Ethical concerns were voiced about 'saving' arrests for a high profile operation on a pre-determined date on the grounds that individuals, against whom there was sufficient evidence on which to base an arrest, were free to commit more crimes in the intervening period. Furthermore, some evidence may be time-sensitive and its value may be diminished by delay.

Recent 1 Area initiatives: The 'stop and speak' campaign was seen to conflict with the style of local policing and officers were apprehensive that such activity could be construed as harassment and would therefore lead to increased tension on the streets. Warning residents about burglaries using a public address system was seen as counter-productive because of its contribution to fear of crime.

Internal communication strategies

Information exchange

Views were divided as to the adequacy of the information provided about Operation Bumblebee. Most officers had some idea of the Operation's aims and were satisfied with the information provided about the Operation, through briefings, leaflets, 'The Job' and via the media. The minority view was that the information had been inadequate, especially that provided to uniformed officers, with the result that they did not feel 'part of Bumblebee' and saw the operation solely as mass searches. Although within the MPS, the Department of Public Affairs (DPA) had been active in its support and promotion of Bumblebee, officers' responses suggested that its success had been somewhat limited and that the information had not always reached its target audience nor had stimulated active involvement.

Three-quarters of the officers interviewed in Gloucestershire were content with the information they had received about Operation Gemini which they felt had provided a clear idea of Gemini's aims. In Hampshire, a wide variation in officers' familiarity with the content of the Review of the Investigation of Crime and the CID, combined with the lack of a high-profile strategy for combating burglary in Hampshire, led to a more diffuse set of responses. While the majority of officers were conversant with the Review's content, one in seven had little or no idea of its aims and effects.

There was little evidence in any of the forces of a formal communication strategy appropriate to its size and structure or means of monitoring the effectiveness of internal communication about the force's anti-burglary strategy. In all three cases, considerable effort had been devoted to strategy development but comparatively little attention appeared to have been paid to the need for internal marketing, especially at a local level, to maximise officers' involvement.

Officers at headquarters and at area level (MPS), and those with a specific responsibility for burglary were most likely to be involved in policy discussions, briefings etc. which provided a forum in which they could express their views about the way burglary should be addressed. However, one in three officers had been given no opportunity to contribute their views, and junior officers attached to burglary squads and beat/sector officers involved in service delivery, especially those in the MPS, would have welcomed more chance to contribute and to comment on management proposals.

Performance feedback

In all three forces, officers felt that performance feedback could be improved considerably. Most of those interviewed in the MPS and in Gloucestershire had received some feedback on the impact of their respective operations from both formal and informal internal sources, the media, the public (especially victims), other agencies (eg. local authorities) and criminals. The response from the media, victims and other agencies was uniformly perceived as positive. Feedback from criminals was mixed. In Hampshire, feedback was restricted mainly to statistical information, and officers of all ranks commented on the poor flow of information in general within the force. Some senior officers in Hampshire were seeking feedback from customers via victim surveys and other research.

Access to crime statistics varied with an officer's rank and role and was particularly limited in Hampshire, with officers with no management role receiving very little or no feedback on local or force performance with respect to burglary. Other than in the MPS, there was little indication that the amount or availability of statistical information had increased recently, and there was considerable scope for making such information more accessible and improving its presentation.

Media publicity

In both the MPS and Gloucestershire, the dominant reaction to the publicity campaigns for their respective operations was positive. In the MPS, publicity was seen as valuable in raising public awareness of burglary and of the police response to the problem. Senior officers in Gloucestershire emphasised the role of publicity, especially coverage in local newspapers, in overcoming public apathy and inspiring neighbourhood watches.

Only a minority of officers were openly critical, although a number considered the campaigns needed revitalizing because they were losing their impact. In both the MPS and Gloucestershire, the major criticisms were that the campaigns fail to reach sufficient people, raise expectations which cannot be met, increase the fear of crime unnecessarily, and warn criminals of police activity. Additionally within the MPS, some officers disliked the Bumblebee logo and imagery, while others took the view that the campaign failed to provide the public with sufficiently detailed crime prevention information. Some officers also felt that the campaign was too area-led, and took no account of local risk levels and associated fear of crime. Questions were also raised about whether the cost of the publicity campaign could be justified and whether it offered value for money. Most areas had undertaken local publicity initiatives to compensate for the campaign's deficiencies.

In Hampshire there had been no high-profile media campaign of the kind that existed in the MPS and Gloucestershire. The majority of officers interviewed in Hampshire felt that the force should do considerably more to inform the public and other agencies of their efforts to combat burglary, both in order to reduce the fear of crime and to emphasise that crime is a community, not just a police, problem. Officers did comment on the force's good relations with both the press and local radio, and their use of the media to highlight major problems and occasional special operations. Close liaison with neighbourhood watches, for example informing local co-ordinators about the incidence of burglaries, was considered to be a vital element in combating burglary in the county.

Level of support

The dominant view of Operation Bumblebee was positive. Officers saw it as good operational strategy, based on the principles of proactive policing, targeting of known criminals, and improved use of criminal intelligence and CPA and, in most cases, the use of dedicated squads. It had served to promulgate good practice and to counteract parochialism. The operation was seen to have brought results and to be good for police morale. Its high profile had focused attention on burglary and demonstrated to the public that action was being taken. The significant minority who were negative voiced a number of criticisms. Many considered that Bumblebee had been ineffective and regarded it as 'merely' a public relations exercise. On both areas, there was criticism of the 'Bumblebee days' (simultaneous searches and arrests) and some disquiet about the focus on PSVs.

Operation Gemini was clearly popular. Three out of four officers considered Gemini was achieving its aims, although some of these felt it was only just beginning to have an impact. The remainder commented upon insufficient CID input, lack of resources, some officers' cynicism and diversion of effort from other police work. All the senior officers interviewed were extremely supportive and most felt that the strategy embodied in Gemini had an excellent prospect of controlling the current crime wave.

In Hampshire, although many of the Review's recommendations were endorsed, there were some cogent criticisms. Most officers saw the Review's recommendations as contributing to a more effective and professional response to burglary and other crime. However, there was criticism of both the slow pace and variability of implementation. Stricter control, monitoring and evaluation were seen as essential. Some officers, of all ranks, criticised the fact that the Review had been conducted internally - indeed by the CID itself - rather than by external consultants, and had failed to address the fundamental question of the role of the CID. It was seen as providing a framework, rather than a strategy, for crime investigation, or as merely restating much of what was already common practice.

Perceived success

Impact on target domains

Senior officers in Gloucestershire were overwhelmingly positive in their view of the impact of Operation Gemini. Their only concerns were the need for adequate resources - personnel, encrypted radios and vehicles - and the possibility of geographical displacement of crime (especially on Cotswold and Forest divisions). Those from the MPS and Hampshire expressed a wider range of views. Senior officers in the MPS felt that Operation Bumblebee had had some positive impact, especially on the prevention and detection of burglary, the public's image of the police, and on police morale. However, there was concern about the lack of attention to crimes other than burglary and possible displacement.

In Hampshire, senior officers questioned whether the force could be deemed to have a strategy for dealing with burglary and highlighted the essential conflict between the need for coherence and the delegation of control to sub-divisions. The dominant assessment was that the recent reorganisation and changes in operational practice had had little or no impact on the prevention and detection of burglary or other crimes or in any of the other domains. Any changes that were identified, for example, the reduction of 'beauty spot' crime in the New Forest, were attributed to local initiatives rather than to the Review.

The assessments by officers below the rank of chief inspector, who were asked to assess the impact of their force's recent actions in six domains, show substantial variation across forces (Table 7). However, in general, Operations Bumblebee and Gemini were seen to have had a greater and more wide-ranging positive effect than Hampshire's approach to burglary. A substantial minority of officers argued that their force's strategy had had a deleterious effect on police morale and offences other than burglary.

Table 7: Positive impact of the three strategies: number (n) and percentage (%) of officers who expressed a positive view (officers below the rank of chief inspector)

| | | MPS | | Glocs | | Hants | | TOTAL | |
| | | 1 Area | 4 Area | | | | | | |
	Target domain	n (%)	n (%)	n (%)	n (%)	n (%)
a.	Prevention/detection of burglary	28 (88)	28 (80)	25 (81)	16 (62)	97 (78)
b.	Prevention/detection of other offences	16 (59)	15 (41)	13 (38)	11 (58)	55 (47)
c.	Public's image of/cooperation with the police	30 (91)	26 (74)	21 (75)	9 (43)	86 (74)
d.	Cooperation of other agencies with the police	28 (82)	14 (39)	17 (57)	13 (54)	72 (58)
e.	Views/attitudes of criminals	13 (41)	16 (46)	20 (71)	3 (21)	52 (48)
f.	Police motivation/morale	9 (32)	18 (49)	22 (61)	5 (39)	54 (47)

Contributors to and constraints on success

There were certain commonalities across the three forces with respect to those factors which were identified as contributing to the success of their anti-burglary strategies (Table 8). The success of both Bumblebee and Gemini was seen to be heavily dependent upon the media publicity and increased public awareness. Efficient gathering and use of criminal intelligence was believed to be essential in all three forces but was regarded as the key factor in Hampshire's approach. In both Gloucestershire and Hampshire, changes in the management of crime - the introduction of crime management units and crime desks - were seen as extremely valuable.

Table 8: Officers' views: key factors contributing to success in the three forces

	MPS	Glocs	Hants
Media publicity and associated increase in public awareness	x	x	
Allocation/focusing of resources	x	x	x
Dedicated squads/units	x	x	
More active/professional approach	x	x	
More/better use of criminal intelligence	x	x	x
Commitment of officers and senior management	x	x	x
Coherent/integrated strategy with well-defined objectives	x	x	
Establishment of crime management units/crime desks		x	x
Sponsorship from outside organisations		x	
Good forensic support, especially fingerprint identifications		x	
Clearer direction and better defined priorities/responsibilities			x

Similarly, there was considerable consensus about those factors identified as detracting from the success of their strategies, with lack of resources being the most important (Table 9).

Table 9: Officers' views: constraints on success in the three forces

	MPS	Glocs	Hants
Lack of resources - personnel (including depletion of shifts caused by loss of officers to dedicated units), equipment, funds for overtime	x	x	x
Inadequacies of the CJS (eg. lack of custodial sentences)	x	x	x
Insufficient gathering/analysis/use of intelligence (exacerbated by inadequate/incompatible IT systems and software)	x	x	x
Management attitudes and decisions - conflict between local priorities and central prescriptions for action, variable local support/commitment	x		x
Lack of preparation and poor logistical backup		x	

Future developments

Strategy development

The majority view was that the problem of burglary would get worse or, at best, remain at a similar level as today. Officers highlighted problems associated with the CJS (especially sentencing policy), the increasing availability and demand for drugs and the possible effects of unemployment. They also pointed to the fact that increased crime prevention awareness and the designing-out of crime were both slow to impact on burglary figures and that burglars were becoming increasingly sophisticated. Officers in all three forces argued for an increasingly proactive approach supported by appropriate resources. However, it was seen as extremely important that any adopted strategy should be kept under review and adapted to meet changing demands and new priorities - drugs were seen to constitute a major problem which **must** be addressed.

The dominant view in all three forces was that a single approach could be applied to burglary and helped to ensure that good practice was shared. However, officers emphasised that there should be the potential for local flexibility to respond to local priorities and deal with urban/rural differences, and that the strategy should be adequately resourced. Those officers who were against a common approach to burglary, the majority of whom were in Gloucestershire and Hampshire, argued that the problems were so different across different locations as to make a single approach impractical.

Sustainability and applicability to other high-volume crime

The majority view in the MPS and in Gloucestershire was that their respective operations were sustainable in the medium to long-term, provided they were sufficiently resourced, were closely monitored, retained the flexibility necessary to respond to local circumstances and were revitalised by new ideas at regular intervals. Officers who viewed Bumblebee and Gemini merely as short-term operations argued that they had lost their impact and needed relaunching. In the MPS, there was the feeling that the continued use of mass searches and the nature of some working practices (eg. PSVs to offenders with non-custodial sentences) did not contribute to the operation's long-term viability. Moreover, the continual promotion of Bumblebee had resulted in some officers becoming weary of the operation and references to it as 'tedious' or 'Bumblebore' did not bode well for the future.

The dominant view in all three forces was that the strategic elements of Operations Bumblebee and Gemini and of Hampshire's strategy were generalisable to a range of high-volume crimes, other than burglary, including motor-vehicle crime (already addressed by Gemini), street robbery and, in certain locations, drug offences.

Should Hampshire adopt Operation Bumblebee?

A majority of senior officers and half those below the rank of chief inspector did not favour the introduction of Operation Bumblebee in Hampshire. In their view, the resource demands were too high, the problems in Hampshire too variable (eg. across urban and rural locations) and dissimilar to those faced in the MPD (eg. travelling criminals). They also maintained that such an operation was impossible to sustain in the long-term and a force like Hampshire could not cope with its demands force-wide. They therefore favoured localised operations and short-term initiatives directed at local problems. It was also pointed out that Hampshire had already benefited from adopting many of the practices associated with Bumblebee, such as intelligence-based targeting, without exposing themselves to the risks associated with a high-profile operation.

One out of every two officers below the rank of chief inspector would like to see a Bumblebee-type operation introduced in Hampshire, but only if it was appropriately resourced, well-planned and supported, and relevant to local problems and patterns of activity.

Other benefits

Operational practice and organisation

All three approaches have brought about changes in operational practice and organisational structures so as to increase proactivity. The anti-burglary strategies in the MPS and in Gloucestershire had helped to emphasise the role of proactivity in controlling this category of crime. However, such a shift in emphasis is primarily affected by the organisation and responsibilities of squads, the development of an integrated system for the gathering, analysis and dissemination of intelligence, and allocation of resources. All three strategies had addressed these issues although none had yet achieved the desired balance between proactive and reactive work.

The existence of a well-defined strategy does not necessarily imply uniformity of action. Hampshire showed considerable variation in strategy implementation and working practice and some variation was also evident in the MPS, despite the guidelines associated with Operation Bumblebee. The variation in these two cases partly reflects the larger size, longer chains of command and greater impact of local control in these two forces in comparison with Gloucestershire.

Support and commitment

Key issues which have affected the implementation process are the mismatch between resource demands and availability, and the level of officers' support for the strategy and its associated structural and procedural changes. Although all three strategies enjoyed support from the majority of officers, Bumblebee and Gemini received a more favourable response. Both operations had a clear advantage over Hampshire's approach by having well-defined objectives. However, Bumblebee, which is the most directive of the three strategies, generated concerns about its prescriptive nature, and highlights the fundamental problem of central versus local control.

Improvements in motivation and morale can be valuable additional benefits of a defined anti-crime strategy, but are unlikely to be gained unless the strategy is marketed effectively within an organisation. Although there was evidence that the existence of a coherent strategy had had an impact on the morale of officers, none of the forces had implemented a comprehensive programme of internal communications to ensure that all officers and civil staff were fully aware of the strategy, its objectives, achievements - and constraints - or the individual contributions expected of them. This was particularly evident in the MPS, where both size and structure make communications problematic.

Service to victims

In all three cases there was evidence of an enhanced quality of service to burglary victims. Officers were more aware of the impact of burglary upon victims and appeared to be more sympathetic and supportive than had previously been the case. Although such changes were evident in Hampshire, Bumblebee and Gemini were more closely associated with a distinct and recognisable cultural shift, which had affected both police attitudes toward burglary and their behaviour toward victims.

Public relations

Officers believe that the publicity campaigns and media coverage given to Bumblebee and Gemini have improved the image of the police in the eyes of the public. Hampshire had no high profile media campaign, and more could be done to persuade the public and other agencies that crime is a community, not just a police problem.

A successful campaign against burglary involves co-operation from other agencies and organisations. Although all three forces provided examples of successful partnerships with a range of external bodies, high profile focused campaigns, such as Bumblebee and Gemini, offered some advantages in developing and sustaining such partnerships. Private sector sponsorship has also been exploited successfully, especially by Gloucestershire. Although the contributions such sponsorship agreements can make to police work are legally and ethically constrained, if they are deemed to be appropriate then their development is facilitated by a targeted strategy aimed at improving quality of life.

The publicity campaigns and positive media coverage associated with Bumblebee and Gemini appear to have made valuable contributions to raising the profile of burglary, increasing awareness of police action to combat the problem and emphasising community responsibility for the control of crime.

Drawbacks

No strategy, successful or otherwise, is without its drawbacks and these need to be addressed if a strategy is to be sustained and developed.

Prioritising burglary

Both Bumblebee and Gemini, but particularly Bumblebee, are open to the possibility that their restricted focus will result in pressure to achieve performance targets with respect to burglary, at the expense of crime control in other areas or quality of service. Moreover, activities which target a crime such as burglary may result in the public perception - or indeed that of criminals - that the police pay less attention to crimes other than burglary. At this stage, there is little indication that this is so in either case, but this must be kept under review. The decision not to prioritise burglary force-wide enables Hampshire to respond to local priorities, but is not without some disadvantages. There is no defined strategy for dealing with burglary and this results in a lack of focus.

Limited applicability

So far, Bumblebee appears to have had a greater effect on burglary than Gemini. This difference in performance, combined with the pattern of high-volume crime observed in Gloucestershire, suggests that a high-profile operation, coupled with a proactive approach, is more successful in urban than rural areas. Where population is sparse and criminals are mobile, targeting of offenders will be less effective and covert surveillance of individuals more difficult. However, both Hampshire and Gloucestershire have enjoyed some success with ingenious surveillance operations which targeted high risk locations.

Sustainability

The analysis of the two 'brand name' operations against burglary shows that they are heavily dependent upon committed leadership and support at all levels within the police service. These key elements in both the internal and external promotion of the two strategies will need to be maintained if the operations are to sustain their impact.

Operations which are reliant upon media publicity require a regular supply of innovative ideas to retain their vitality and publicity value. Gemini, with its changing focus and related publicity themes, has addressed this issue and the operation's dual focus gives considerable scope for developing its publicity and media coverage in the future. In the case of Bumblebee, it may be more difficult both to generate new ideas which officers regard as good practice and to sustain the level of media coverage it has enjoyed in the past. Hampshire's approach is less dependent upon the innovation necessary to generate external publicity, which may offer an advantage in terms of its long-term viability.

There is an obvious danger that high-profile strategies, although they may have a dramatic effect initially, will not make a long-term contribution to the reduction of crime. The three approaches - whether high-profile or otherwise - all emphasise, to varying degrees, the importance of measures to encourage crime prevention, both by means of operational changes and by eliciting public involvement and inter-agency cooperation. At this stage, it remains an open question - especially in the case of the two high-profile strategies - whether these measures either are sufficient to achieve their aims or are sustainable, since the time period of the evaluation was necessarily too limited to draw firm conclusions about the long-term impact of the three strategies.

Resource distribution

A strategy directed at burglary necessarily entails a redistribution of resources. In all three cases, but particularly in the MPS and in Gloucestershire, resources had been allocated to burglary, which necessarily meant reductions for other areas of activity. Although at this early stage of the operations there was no firm indication of reduced performance elsewhere, care must be taken to ensure that long-term operations against burglary do not unduly distort the deployment of available resources.

Additional costs

The available information was insufficient to carry out a detailed analysis of the costs associated with the three strategies and therefore of their cost-effectiveness. Apart from an additional overtime budget for Gemini I, Gloucestershire had not allocated any additional funds to Operation Gemini, the costs of the Gemini publicity campaign being met mainly by private sponsorship. Neither had Hampshire provided any additional funding for the prevention and detection of burglary. In the case of Bumblebee, although it is possible to cost the publicity campaign, attempts to estimate the opportunity costs associated with the operation are at a very early stage, and neither give a clear picture of the additional costs incurred. Any extra activity directed at burglary, even though it may have no implications for total expenditure, must involve a shift of resources from some other area of activity, if only at the local level. It is unfortunate that in the case of the two strategies which target burglary, these costs have not been identified so as to permit an informative value for money analysis.

4. Implications for good practice

The analysis of the strategies adopted by the three police services has demonstrated that they have had some success in the fight against high-volume crime. It is unlikely that any one element described in this report is unique to any of the participating forces: many will have been implemented, with varying degrees of success, elsewhere. Similarly, other forces will have developed their own strategies from which officers in London, Gloucestershire and Hampshire might usefully learn. However, the current study has clear implications for 'good practice' which are summarised below.

Publicity

The experience of both the MPS and Gloucestershire Constabulary suggests that a high profile named operation can bring a number of advantages. A 'brand name' is an important feature in that:

- It provides a unifying focus to a range of activities - it helps to illustrate how they can be linked and co-ordinated to achieve defined objectives and can have a beneficial effect on police morale.
- It makes police operations understandable to the public - it helps to reassure the public that the police share their concerns and are seeking to improve their performance.

There is, however, an important caveat. Publicity should not be over-optimistic; care should be taken to ensure that expectations are not raised beyond the level that can reasonably be met. Care should also be exercised in the use of a 'brand name' so that its impact is not dissipated. It should be borne in mind that people can grow contemptuous of the familiar. Thus, the brand name of a high profile operation should be kept under review and the attitudes of both police officers and the public should be monitored. The fact that officers perceive the high level of media publicity to make a major contribution to the success of both Bumblebee and Gemini implies that, if the operations fail to attract such publicity in the future, then the commitment of officers may be diminished. If a brand name loses its impact, it should be relaunched, or abandoned and replaced.

A high profile campaign, emphasising a partnership between police and public, may attract support, including sponsorship from the private sector. Subject to current legal constraints, anything which adds to public service without cost to public funds must be welcome but such relationships could prove embarrassing if the probity of the company were to be called into question. Sponsorship should only be accepted when potential sponsors have satisfied the necessary conditions.

An improvement in public relations is inherently valuable but is not an end in itself. Care should be taken to ensure that an enhanced public image of the police leads to concrete benefits. Both the MPS and Gloucestershire have exploited the 'image' of their respective high profile operations to raise public awareness of crime and the contribution the public can make to both its prevention and detection. Local initiatives involving partnerships with local authorities and other agencies and organisations have proved invaluable. Such work is not entirely dependent upon a named strategy, as Hampshire has demonstrated, but having a 'brand name' provides a framework. The advantage of Bumblebee and Gemini is that they provide a convenient label for the socially acceptable face of crime prevention and detection, with which both the public and other agencies wish to be associated.

The yield from this activity has been to encourage action by others to support the police in their crime prevention and detection work. Local housing authorities, builders and housing associations have begun to look at ways of 'designing out' crime by improving estate layouts, lighting and security, and ordinary citizens have been brought together to form more Neighbourhood Watches. Improved public goodwill can also make a valuable contribution to intelligence gathering. If the public have faith and trust in the police, and recognise both the efforts being made and the results achieved, they are more inclined to provide useful information.

Internal communication

An effective communication and consultation system is vital in ensuring the successful implementation of any strategy and in encouraging officers' commitment and support. It is apparent from the research that strategies - high profile or otherwise - can only be effective if they are adequately communicated. Where there were communication deficiencies, the research team encountered a degree of disaffection and cynicism.

Officers are likely to be more committed and effective when they are fully informed about the objectives and methods of an operation and, most important of all, about their individual roles and responsibilities within it. A strategy must be clearly set out and its implementation should be preceded by a carefully prepared internal communications exercise to ensure that each and every officer is fully aware of what is expected of her or him. Informal briefings are not adequate for this purpose: not all officers, even those with command experience, are expert communicators. A communications exercise which is both centrally devised and executed must be supported at a local level, especially where there are potential conflicts between central and local power and control.

Care should also be taken to provide opportunities for consultation, so that officers have the chance to contribute at the planning stage. Good ideas often originate at the lower working levels of organisations and those who have contributed to strategy development are more likely to be enthusiastic about its implementation.

Continued involvement is more likely if officers at all levels are kept informed of progress and the information provided not only highlights successes but also recognises difficulties. Regular printed material, such as newsletters, is a useful addition to traditional, informal methods, but it must be attractively presented and widely circulated.

Training

The research identified a number of areas in which further training could be valuable in ensuring the success of an anti-burglary strategy. Consideration should be given at the planning stage to training needs. Members of dedicated teams, particularly those seconded from shifts or sectors, would benefit from training in surveillance methods and the recruitment and handling of informants. Officers with responsibilities for the recording and analysis of criminal intelligence and identification of crime patterns should be trained to use available IT. The responsibilities of the first officer at the scene of a crime need emphasis. First officers at the scene, often uniformed constables, should be aware that their role is to initiate an investigation, not simply to note and report. Appropriate action by these officers, such as scene preservation and local inquiries, can make a useful contribution to the detection of a crime, and reassures victims that action is being taken.

Service to victims of burglary

There have already been improvements in the quality of service provided to victims. These need to be sustained and should not be eroded by pressures to improve more tangible performance indicators.

Common elements of good practice include:

- A prompt *response* to all reported burglaries - not necessarily attendance.
- Prompt *attendance* in cases where the victim is elderly or infirm, alone or distressed.
- Sympathetic and caring behaviour by the first officer at the scene and by other officers involved in the investigation.
- Advice about local victim support services and contact arrangements.
- A realistic assessment of the chances of recovering property and apprehending the perpetrator.
- Crime prevention follow-up to avoid repeat victimisation.
- Follow-up contact to advise the victim of what police action has been taken and the outcome of any investigations.

Another practice worthy of wider use was first officers at the scene supplying householders with telephone numbers of a selection of reputable locksmiths, carpenters and glaziers, to help victims, who often feel vulnerable and uncertain whom to trust, take immediate steps to resecure their property.

Crime prevention

One aim of an anti-burglary strategy is to stimulate public interest and encourage crime prevention measures. To meet the demand thus generated, and to ensure the take-up of crime prevention advice, attention should be paid to the status, location and integration of the crime prevention service. CPOs should be of sufficient status to deal effectively with both external agencies and the public, and to gain access to police resources. Closer relationships among CPOs, crime managers and specialist units are essential to ensure crime prevention initiatives are co-ordinated with other activities. Crime prevention must not be seen as the 'poor relation', but as an integral part of an anti-burglary strategy.

Equipment and support services

The value of adequate and appropriate equipment, especially for specialist teams and covert operations, cannot be over-emphasised. The ready availability of scanning equipment makes encrypted radios essential. 'Covert' vehicles are often recognisable as police vehicles - especially if they are the same make and colour and have sequential registration numbers. Frequent changes of vehicles, by means of interchange within forces, or by short-term leasing, could help to overcome this problem.

Information technology remains problematic. A more proactive approach requires greater availability of both computer hardware and software for the recording, analysis and dissemination of criminal intelligence and crime trends and of appropriate officers trained in its use. More standardisation of systems, both within and across forces, would facilitate the sharing of information. Modern computer systems are generally easy to use and knowledge of their use should not be restricted to specialist officers. Those who gather intelligence, including uniformed officers, are likely to be more effective if they understand how the information is stored, accessed and manipulated. Furthermore, the return on investment in IT is reduced if only a handful of officers are trained to use a system and it stands idle during periods of abstraction, leave or sickness.

An increase in the number of burglary offences solved is heavily dependent upon the contributions made by SOCOs and forensic science units. A sufficient number of SOCOs must be available, and this raises the question of whether their skills should be more widely disseminated so as to offer a more streamlined service to victims. Also, forensic science units must have the capacity for coping with the required number of forensic identifications and offering the necessary speed of response. Automated fingerprint identification is an essential element in this process.

The proactive approach

For a proactive, intelligence-based approach to play an increasing role in combating crime requires more than a mere statement of policy. Increased proactivity requires enhanced collection, analysis and dissemination of criminal intelligence and crime patterns, and appropriate structures and support systems to ensure that proactive capacity is not eroded by reactive demands.

Criminal intelligence

Identification and targeting of active criminals requires an integrated and well-supervised intelligence system. Officers should be fully briefed about the features of the proactive approach and regularly reminded of the system for recording and passing on intelligence information. The 'adopt a burglar' scheme, whereby beat/sector officers are asked to take a particular interest in a criminal, enables uniformed officers to contribute to the collection of intelligence. Intelligence gathering can also be enhanced by increased reliance on informants but their use is dependent upon the availability both of officers trained in their recruitment and handling, and of funds for payment.

Crime pattern analysis

CPA can yield useful information about the likely locations and times of high volume crime. In many cases, CPA has been used to guide the deployment of resources, but its potential value has not been fully exploited; staffing levels and distribution of resources sometimes fail to reflect patterns and amount of criminal activity. However, in some locations, especially metropolitan areas, the volume and distribution of crime is such that the resources are insufficient to target all high risk areas. Targeting active criminals and high risk areas is dependent upon the generation of actionable intelligence and a well-resourced surveillance capability. Until these requirements are met, the policy of an intelligence-led, proactive response will not be achieved in practice.

Specialist squads

The establishment of specialist squads is generally seen as good practice and as fundamental to taking a more proactive approach. The primary benefits come from the concentration of specialist knowledge, skills and related expertise. In principle, a squad can provide a committed resource, protected from day-to-day concerns which might, otherwise, distract attention from the targeted crimes. A major question is whether there should be dedicated burglary squads - as with Bumblebee - or whether specialist teams should deal with more than one category of crime, for example, burglary and motor-vehicle crime - as with Gemini - or whether burglary should be dealt with by a general crime, or crime and drugs, unit - as in Hampshire.

The decision is affected by the priority given to burglary in the overall crime strategy, and it is unlikely that a high profile anti-burglary strategy could be successful without specialist units for whom burglary is a major responsibility.

Specialist teams whose responsibilities cover both proactive and reactive work face an obvious difficulty. The pressures of responding to reported crime all too often result in a lack of balance, with the reactive demands taking precedence over a proactive response. There is evidence to favour a separation of proactive and reactive responsibilities. The level within the organisation at which this separation occurs will depend upon organisational and administrative structures in individual forces. The creation of separate proactive and reactive units demands, however, close co-operation in the exchange of information and liaison on operational matters.

There are disadvantages associated with specialist squads. Crimes which lie within their remit may be seen solely as the squad's responsibility, with other officers taking little or no interest. Long term service on a squad can lead to elitism. There should be rotation of officers to ensure that squads are seen as an integral and accountable part of the service, and close liaison with both CID and uniformed officers. In some cases, specialist units may not be the most appropriate structure. It may be more productive to create local CID teams, to work closely with uniformed officers to both facilitate local service provision and encourage the view that dealing with crime is the responsibility of *all* officers, not just specialist squads. However, such a structure can be vulnerable to the impact of abstractions.

Setting objectives and levels of control

The setting of policing objectives, both by the Home Secretary and by individual forces, has tended to stress tangible performance indicators, such as speed of response to incidents and minimum clear-up targets. Not only are national and local objectives not always congruent with each other, but also an emphasis on the more obvious and most easily measured aspects of police performance can be seen to conflict with the requirement to give the best quality of service to victims. Officers therefore receive mixed messages about what are the 'real' priorities. Senior management must recognise these concerns and give guidance and support to local management and those involved in service delivery. They must also ensure that pressure for performance with respect to targeted crimes, such as burglary, does not lead to a reduction in performance with respect to other offences, or in the co-operation with other forces in dealing with cross-border crime. Furthermore, performance targets, while encouraging administrative efficiency in recording offences and clear-ups, can promote changes in recording and other work practices which may be open to question. Both policy statements and quality control mechanisms are necessary to ensure that integrity is a not a casualty of the pursuit of improvements in performance.

There is also a conflict between a centrally directed strategy and devolution of operational control. A centrally generated strategy for combating burglary needs to be flexible enough to respond to local priorities and to incorporate local initiatives. It should act as a framework for innovation rather than constrain local commanders' ability to respond to local concerns. Freedom to respond to neighbourhood issues helps to ensure that such a strategy is not perceived as over-prescriptive.

Crime management

An effective anti-burglary strategy needs to be coupled with an efficient system of crime management, for example, by establishing crime management units or crime desks, to ensure effective deployment of resources and a co-ordinated response. The criteria which determine the extent of an investigation need to be explicit and consistent, but their application will reflect individual circumstances, local community priorities and resource levels. These structures and systems enable crime managers/ evaluators to ensure an appropriate initial response and to monitor the progress of an investigation. Crime managers also have a key role to play in ensuring that victims receive appropriate support and information. Such a system of crime evaluation and allocation, allied with the establishment of specialist squads, is an effective use of resources and can help to sustain the level of proactivity necessary for the success of an anti-burglary strategy.

5. Conclusions

Burglary is high on the agenda for police action. Officers at all levels are conscious of its prevalence and the often devastating effects upon victims. Anti-burglary strategies therefore command support within the service. Officers will not, however, give their full endorsement to a strategy which, in their view, conflicts with local priorities for resource allocation. Such concerns need to be monitored if anti-burglary strategies are to be sustained at a time when the police service is faced with increasing and competing demands.

Although it is impossible to determine the magnitude of the effects - direct or indirect - of police action, there is evidence that certain strategy changes can contribute to improved performance, as indexed by the recorded incidence and detection of burglary. The introduction of each of the three strategies under examination is associated with improved performance with respect to burglary. The improvements registered by the MPS under the auspices of Operation Bumblebee, which is the most mature of the three strategies, are particularly noteworthy, but there are recent indications that both Hampshire's approach to burglary and Operation Gemini in Gloucestershire are beginning to make a contribution to the control and management of burglary.

Since the introduction of Met-wide Bumblebee, the incidence of recorded burglary has fallen significantly. Also, the number and proportion of burglary offences solved have increased. Although the dramatic improvement in detection performance derives more from secondary than primary clear-ups, the rate of primary clear-ups has improved.

Both Operation Gemini and Hampshire's approach to burglary display some very positive features, but neither has yet achieved its full potential. Operation Gemini and other changes in Gloucestershire have resulted in a small decrease in the incidence of burglary. Although initially the effect appeared to be restricted to primarily urban areas, there is now evidence of a reduction in rural areas. More recently, there is also evidence in Gloucestershire of an increase in the number of burglary offences which are detected, particularly by primary means. In Hampshire, the structural and procedural changes have been slow to take effect. There is now some evidence of a reduction in burglary comparable with that recorded in the MPD, but initial indications of an increase in the number of burglary offences detected do not appear to have been sustained. There is some preliminary evidence of an increase in the number of secondary detections for burglary.

Although there is little evidence of displacement of criminal activity within the MPD, there is some suggestion that displacement may have occurred in Gloucestershire. Crime patterns need to be closely monitored to determine whether the sustained targeting of a particular crime in a given area results in either geographical or category displacement.

Comparisons across the three strategies suggest:

- A high public profile can serve to enhance and accelerate the effects of structural and organisational changes designed to focus resources and produce a more active and effective response to burglary.
- A targeted, proactive strategy is likely to be more effective in an urban environment.
- A more global focus on crime investigation - with flexibility in priorities and the focusing of resources but still emphasising a more proactive, intelligence-based approach - although slower to take effect, can be equally effective, especially where the range of problems and policing contexts are heterogeneous.
- Improvements in the number of detections of burglary are attributable to increases in the number of secondary detections, especially those arising from post-sentence visits including, in the case of the MPS, post-sentence visits to those with non-custodial sentences.

The determinants of levels of crime - including burglary - and associated detection performance are multiple and complex. Although many of these determinants lie outside the ambit of any policing activity, innovative strategies which contain certain key elements can contribute to the control of crime and its detection. However, there is no single police action which alone can reduce the incidence of burglary, increase the rate of detection or improve the quality of service to the public. Successful strategies combine a number of components, some of which are features of all three cases examined.

Key elements of a successful anti-burglary strategy include:

- Clearly defined, internally consistent objectives.
- A proactive, intelligence-based approach.
- Adequate, targeted resources.
- Appropriate structures and acceptable work practices.
- An effective publicity campaign and positive media coverage.
- Multi-agency co-operation.
- A crime management system which ensures an appropriate, co-ordinated response to reported burglaries and an efficient, supportive service to victims.
- Local flexibility.

Lack of resources is seen by officers to be the major constraint on full strategy implementation. There are also concerns about the increasing emphasis on post-sentence visits. Views about solving offences in this way and the associated resource demands will continue to be the subject of debate.

High profile strategies, such as Bumblebee and Gemini, bring additional benefits. A strategy with a 'brand name' generates publicity, helps to inspire public confidence, motivates officers and transfers fear of crime from the victim to the offender. However, media attention should not generate unrealistic public expectations.

All of the three strategies would benefit from better internal marketing. None of the three police forces had developed a fully effective internal communications system in relation to the strategy and its impact. It is vital to 'sell' a strategy to those involved in service delivery so that officers enjoy some degree of ownership and involvement.

The effectiveness of an anti-burglary strategy is likely to be enhanced if there is scope for local initiatives to take account of varying needs and priorities.

The strategic elements of a high-profile, proactive approach to burglary could be applied to other categories of high volume crime, especially motor vehicle crime.

In the longer term, there must be doubts about the sustainability of high-profile, targeted operations unless they are closely monitored and revitalised at appropriate intervals.

The increasing emphasis on results, as reflected in tangible performance indicators, rather than process, which places pressures on all forces irrespective of their strategy for dealing with burglary, must be the subject of continuing scrutiny to ensure that integrity, quality of service and other areas of police activity are not casualties of the quest for attainment of performance targets.

The timing of this evaluation means that the external and internal effects of these three approaches to combating burglary should be re-examined at a later date if more definitive conclusions are to be drawn about their long-term contribution to the control and management of crime and their cost-effectiveness.

References

Audit Commission (1990) *Effective Policing: Performance Review in Police Forces.* London: HMSO.

Dixon B. & Stanko E. (1993) *Serving the People. Sector policing and public accountability.* Islington Council.

Field, S. (1990) *Trends in crime and their interpretation: a study of recorded crime in England and Wales.* Home Office Research Study 119. London: HMSO.

Gloucestershire Constabulary (1992) *The Chief Constable's Annual Report, 1992.*

Hampshire Constabulary (1992) *Hampshire Constabulary Annual Report, 1992.*

HMIC (1987) HMIC's letter of 30 January 1987 to Chief Officers.

Home Office (1993) *Digest 2. Information on the Criminal Justice System in England and Wales.* Home Office Research and Statistics Department.

Home Office (1994) *Notifiable Offences. England and Wales, July 1993 to June 1994.* Home Office Statistical Bulletin. Issue 24/94.

Mayhew, P. and Aye Maung, N. (1992) *Surveying Crime: Findings from the 1992 British Crime Survey.* Home Office Research and Statistics Department, No. 2. October 1992.

Mayhew, P., Mirrlees-Black, C. and Aye Maung, N. (1994) *Trends in Crime: Findings from the 1994 British Crime Survey.* Home Office Research and Statistics Department. Research Findings No. 14. September 1994.

Metropolitan Police (1994) *Recording Crimes and Clear-ups. Guidance and good practice for investigators.*

CRIME PREVENTION UNIT SERIES PAPERS

1. **Reducing Burglary: a study of chemists' shops.** Gloria Laycock. 1985.

2. **Reducing Crime: developing the role of crime prevention panels.** Lorna J. F. Smith and Gloria Laycock. 1985.

3. **Property Marking: a deterrent to domestic burglary?** Gloria Laycock. 1985.

4. **Designing for Car Security: towards a crime free car.** Dean Southall and Paul Ekblom. 1986.

5. **The Prevention of Shop Theft: an approach through crime analysis.** Paul Ekblom. 1986.

6. **Prepayment Coin Meters: a target for burglary.** Nigel Hill. 1986.

7. **Crime in Hospitals: diagnosis and prevention.** Lorna J. F. Smith.

8. **Preventing Juvenile Crime: the Staffordshire Experience.** Kevin Heal and Gloria Laycock. 1987.

9. **Preventing Robberies at Sub-Post Offices: an evaluation of a security initiative.** Paul Ekblom. 1987.

10. **Getting the Best out of Crime Analysis.** Paul Ekblom. 1988.

11. **Retail Crime: Prevention through Crime Analysis.** John Burrows. 1988.

12. **Neighbourhood Watch in England and Wales: a locational analysis.** Sohail Husain. 1988.

13. **The Kirkholt Burglary Prevention Project, Rochdale.** David Forrester, Mike Chatterton and Ken Pease with the assistance of Robin Brown. 1988.

14. **The Prevention of Robbery at Building Society Branches.** Claire Austin. 1988.

15. **Crime Prevention and Racial Harassment in Asian-run Small Shops: the scope for prevention.** Paul Ekblom and Frances Simon with the assistance of Sneh Birdi. 1988.

16. **Crime and Nuisance in the Shopping Centre: a case study in crime prevention.** Susan Phillips and Raymond Cochrane. 1988.

17. **The Prevention of Fraud.** Michael Levi. 1988.

18. **An Evaluation of Domestic Security Surveys.** Gloria Laycock. 1989.

19. **Downtown Drinkers: the perceptions and fears of the public in a city centre.** Malcolm Ramsey. 1989.

20. **The Management and Prevention of Juvenile Crime Problems.** Barrymore Cooper. 1989.

21. **Victim Support and Crime Prevention in an Inner-City Setting.** Alice Sampson and Graham Farrell. 1990.

22. **Lagerland Lost? An experiment in keeping Drinkers off the street in central Coventry and elsewhere.** Malcolm Ramsey. 1990.

23. **The Kirkholt Burglary Prevention Project: Phase II.** David Forrester, Samantha Frenz, Martin O'Connell and Ken Pease. 1990.

24. **Probation Practice in Crime Prevention.** Jane Geraghty. 1991.

25. **Lessons from a Victim Support Crime Prevention Project.** Alice Sampson. 1991.

26. **The Prevention of Cheque and Credit Card Fraud.** Michael Levi, Paul Bissell and Tony Richardson. 1991.

27. **Making Crime Prevention Pay: initiatives from business.** John Burrows. 1991.

28. **The Influence of Street Lighting on Crime and Fear of Crime.** Stephen Atkins, Sohail Husain and Angele Storey. 1991.

29. **The Effect of Better Street Lighting on Crime and Fear: a Review.** Malcolm Ramsay with the assistance of Rosemary Newton. 1991.

30. **Reducing Crime on the London Underground.** Barry Webb and Gloria Laycock. 1992.

31. **Assessing Crime Prevention Initiatives: The First Steps.** Geoff Berry and Mike Carter. 1992.

32. **Tackling Car Crime.** Barry Webb and Gloria Laycock. 1992.

33. **Car Theft in England and Wales: The Home Office Car Theft Index.** George Houghton. 1992.

34. **Preventing Car Crime in Car Parks.** Barry Webb, Ben Brown and Katherine Bennett. 1992.

35. **Closed Circuit Television in Public Places.** Terry Honess and Elizabeth Charman. 1992.

36. **Multiple Victimisation: Racial Attacks on an East London Estate.** Alice Sampson and Coretta Phillips. 1992.

37. **Theft and Loss from UK Libraries: A National Survey.** John Burrows and Diane Cooper. 1992.

38. **Safer Cities and Community Safety Strategies.** Nick Tilley. 1992.

39. **Community Service and Crime Prevention: the Cheadle Heath Project.** Mary Barker, Ken Pease and Barry Webb. 1992.

40. **Car Crime and Young People on a Sunderland Housing Estate.** Eileen Spencer. 1993.

41. **Developing Police Crime Prevention: Management and Organisational Change.** Valerie Johnston, Joanna Shapland and Paul Wiles. 1993.

42. **Understanding Car Parks, Crime and CCTV: Evaluation Lessons from Safer Cities.** Nick Tilley. 1993.

43. **Kerb-Crawling, Prostitution and Multi-Agency Policing.** Roger Matthews. 1993.

44. **The Prevention of Street Robbery.** Mary Barker, Jane Geraghty, Barry Webb and Tom Key. 1993.

45. **The Prevention of Crime Against Small Businesses: The Safer Cities Experience.** Nick Tilley. 1993.

46. **Once Bitten, Twice Bitten: Repeat Victimisation and its Implications for Crime Prevention.** Graham Farrell and Ken Pease. 1993.

47. **After Kirkholt – Theory, Method and Results of Replication Evaluations.** Nick Tilley. 1993.

48. **Preventing Domestic Violence to Women.** Rebecca Morley and Audrey Mullender. 1994.

49. **Preventing Repeated Domestic Violence: A Demonstration Project on Merseyside.** Sam Lloyd, Graham Farrell and Ken Pease. 1994.

50. **Vehicle Watch and Car Theft: An Evaluation.** Terry Honess, Michael Maguire and Elizabeth Charman. 1994.

51. **Burglary Reduction: Findings from Safer Cities Schemes.** Nick Tilley and Janice Webb. 1994.

52. **Inter-Agency Crime Prevention: Organising Local Delivery.** Mark Liddle and Loraine Gelsthorpe. 1994.

53. **Crime Prevention and Inter-Agency Cooperation.** Mark Liddle and Loraine Gelsthorpe. 1994

   Inter-Agency Crime Prevention: Further Issues *(Supplementary Paper to Crime Prevention Unit Papers 52 & 53).*

54. **Crime on Industrial Estates.** Valerie Johnston, Maria Leitner, Joanna Shapland & Paul Wiles. 1994.

CRIME DETECTION AND PREVENTION SERIES PAPERS

55. **Witness Intimidation: Strategies for prevention.** Warwick Maynard. 1994.

56. **Preventing Vandalism: What Works?** Mary Barker and Cressida Bridgeman. 1994.

57. **Thinking About Crime Prevention Performance Indicators.** Nick Tilley. 1995.

58. **Biting Back: Tackling Repeat Burglary and Car Crime.** David Anderson, Sylvia Chenery and Ken Pease. 1995.

POLICE RESEARCH SERIES PAPERS

1. **Video Taping Police Interviews with Police Suspects – an Evaluation.** John Baldwin. 1992.

2. **Effective Shift Systems for the Police Service.** Richard Stone, Tim Kemp, Bernard Rix and George Weldon. 1993.

3. **Opportunities for Reducing the Administrative Burdens on the Police.** Paul Cresswell, Graham Howarth, Mike Dolan and John Hedges. 1993.

4. **Investigative Interviewing Courses For Police Officers: An Evaluation.** Barry McGurk, Michael Carr and Debra McGurk. 1993.

5. **Management and Supervision of Police Interviews.** Janet Stockdale. 1993.

6. **Royal Commission Research Papers. A Policing Perspective.** Jane Hirst. 1993.

7. **Part-Time Working and Job Sharing in the Police Service.** Richard Stone, Tim Kemp and George Weldon. 1994.

8. **Managing demand on the Police: An evaluation of a Crime Line.** Chlöe Jolowicz and Tim Read. 1994.

9. **Court Attendance by Police Officers.** Bob Eames, Andrew Hooke and David Portas. 1994.

10. **Assaults on Police Officers: An examination of the circumstances in which such incidents occur.** Ben Brown. 1994.

11. **Assessing the Expandable Side-handled Baton.** Egmont Koch, Tim Kemp and Bernard Rix. 1994.

12. **Traffic Organisation and Activity Study.** Adam Ogilvie-Smith, Elizabeth Ransom and Alan Downey. 1994.